FAMILY FAITH & FUN

Activities, Games, & Prayers for Sharing Faith at Home

Gary J. Boelhower, Ph.D.

HI-TIME Publishing Corporation
Milwaukee, Wisconsin

Use FAMILY FAITH & FUN in the home.

A family will find in this book suggestions for family fun nights, for games that encourage family Scripture sharing, for many ways to celebrate special occasions, for ways to make ordinary times special.

Use FAMILY FAITH & FUN in the faith community.

Pastors, religious educators, teachers, school administrators, and family ministers will find in this book practical ideas to share with families in Sunday bulletin articles, bulletin inserts and mailings, parish and school newsletters, and parent handouts.

Layout and design: Jimmy Hackbarth

HI-TIME Publishing Corporation
1204OL West Feerick Street
Milwaukee, WI 53222
414-466-2420 800-558-2292
FAX 414-461-2920

ISBN 0-937997-29-3

DEDICATION

To those who are FAMILY for me:

To Mom and Dad, for life and the passion to hope and love.

To William, Conrad, Susan, for letting your little brother tag along.

To the Polakowski family and the Giordana family, for modeling family faith
and welcoming me in.

To colleagues in education and ministry throughout the years, for shared insights
and shared commitments to values formation.

To the Maglio family, for family campouts and weekend visits.

To the Rebek family, for sharing family times both profound and trivial.

To the Wahoske family, for traditions and celebrations with good food and good fun.

To my wife, Pat, for an adventure in the deepest kind of friendship and love
that creates a family.

To my children, Rebecca, Joel, Matthew, for not letting me forget
that back rubs and hugs are very important,
that time is the most precious gift,
and that human love is always limited and infinite.

TABLE OF CONTENTS

FAMILY: WHERE FAITH BEGINS AND GROWS

Parents are the first and most important teachers of faith for their children. The family is the critical context within which faith is nurtured and supported. This family context can include grandparents, aunts and uncles, older cousins, and friends as well. Although religious education programs, Christian formation activities, and parochial schools can offer important supplemental experiences and knowledge to build faith, ultimately these programs play only a secondary role. When faith is lived and celebrated and discussed in the home, there is a strong probability that young people will integrate that faith into their own lives as they journey to adulthood. In order to understand more about how faith is communicated in the home, we need to grasp the concept of faith itself.

What is faith? Most people answer this question by defining faith as "belief" or "trust." These two words seem to be the most commonly accepted synonyms for faith. However, neither word defines the essence of faith. Trusting is an emotional expression of faith. A person who has faith often feels that there is a higher power that offers ultimate security. A person can rely on God even when everything else in the person's life is crumbling. Believing is an intellectual expression of faith. A faith-filled person has certain beliefs about who God is and how life is to be lived in relationship with God. Persons who have faith are often called believers. Their beliefs usually include doctrines, teachings, and ethical principles. Although trusting and believing are expressions of faith, they are not faith itself.

To understand the essence of faith, the story of the smuggler might be helpful. John Westerhoff told this story several years ago at the Milwaukee Archdiocesan Religious Education Conference. There was a smuggler who pulled his donkey across the border day after day. Each day the border guards would inspect the donkey and what it carried to try to

---

The family is the critical context within which faith is nurtured and supported.

---

discover the contraband material that the smuggler was sneaking across the border. Everyone knew the smuggler was carrying contraband of some kind because he was getting richer and richer as time went on and he didn't have a job.

Day after day, the smuggler would pull his donkey across the border. The border guards took the straw off the donkey's back and sorted through it piece by piece. They found nothing. The next day, the smuggler would be at the border again, pulling his donkey just as on the day before. The border guards hollowed out the donkey's hooves looking for diamonds, drugs, or maybe even computer chips. They found nothing. On the following day, the smuggler would show up at the border again, pulling his donkey. The border guards pried open that donkey's mouth and inspected every tooth. They found nothing.

Day after day, year after year, the smuggler pulled his donkey across the border. Day after day, year after year, the

Fundamentally, faith is a way of seeing, a mode of perception.

guards tried to find the contraband substance that the smuggler was transporting. They went over every inch of the donkey's hide. They looked under the donkey's eyelids. They inspected the donkey's nostrils. Their inspections increased in intensity and frustration day after day, year after year. Finally, the smuggler decided to retire since he had made all the money he wished or could ever spend in a lifetime. Being a kind man, the smuggler threw a great party for the border guards upon his retirement. After partying all night, the border guards finally got up enough courage to ask the smuggler what he had been smuggling across the border all these years right under their noses. The smuggler smiled at the border guards and said, "Donkeys."

This story illustrates the definition of faith as "a way of seeing." The smuggler and the border guards physically saw the same donkeys day after day. However, the smuggler saw them for what they were and the border guards failed to see their importance or value. Fundamentally, faith is a way of seeing, a mode of perception. To have faith is to see God's presence and power active in the world and one's life. To have faith is to see the world as creation and gift of God. To have faith

is to see others as made in the image of God.

Some people look out at the world and do not see God's presence or power. Like the border guards, those who do not have faith physically see the same world as those who do have faith. Yet, there is a deeper "seeing" that believers have. Believers see God's love and care interwoven in the events of their daily lives. When parents and the extended family pass on faith, they are really passing on a way of seeing reality. In a sense, they enable their children to see with a certain pair of glasses that makes visible the invisible reality of God.

Passing on faith is not ultimately passing on a set of doctrines or teachings or ethical principles, although these are not unimportant. Passing on faith is not ultimately passing on a way of worshiping or celebrating, although symbols and celebrations are key components of the life of faith. At the core, passing on faith means teaching children to see life in a particular way; to glimpse the guiding, loving presence of a God who is involved in life.

If faith is fundamentally "a way of seeing," how is faith communicated in the

Parents need to share their values with their children.

context of the family? Communicating faith is more like the measles than it is like a recipe. In other words, children catch faith more than they learn it like a formula or a concept. Children come to see life in a particular way because people who love them take them by the hand and say, "See!" Parents and members of the extended family take the child by the hand and show the child signs of God's loving presence. Parents take the child for a walk

8

on the shore of a lake and look out at the setting crimson sun and say, "See, how beautiful God's creation is!" Parents take the child by the hand to look at the creche set in front of church and say, "See, Jesus was once a baby like you." Mom or Dad break up a fight with the neighbor kid next door and say, "See, Peter is part of our family, too. All of us are made in God's image. God created everyone." Of course, many times, there are no words necessary to communicate this way of seeing. The warm hug of another person, the smile of recognition, the wide-eyed wondering at the world of nature, all communicate a way of seeing that recognizes God's profound presence in the midst of life. Little by little, the child begins "to see" in a particular way; the child comes to faith.

Passing on the faith is as simple and natural as helping someone see the reality of God. However, teaching someone to see takes time, effort, traditions, stories, discussions, prayers, and service together as family. Passing on the faith will happen differently in every family. There is no recipe or precise set of directions. However, reflection on "coming to see" shows that the process involves several key elements.

1. *Talk about the basement.* The basement of a building is its foundation, the underpinning upon which the entire structure rests. In the same way, our

Teachable moments occur within the context of daily life.

actions and choices are built on the foundation of our values or priorities. So often, parents talk about specific choices they make or wish their children would make, but fail to discuss the reasons why these choices are important. Families need to become more adept at discussing the reasons behind actions and choices. Parents need to share their values with their children. Children often ask "why" because they want to know the basis for

Parents represent the unconditional love of God that is never withdrawn.

certain decisions or family policies. The parental response, "Because I said so!" fails to provide the child with the foundation. Children may not necessarily agree with the particular parental decision, but they are more apt to accept a decision that reflects a value that the parent holds dear. Sharing the values that provide the basis for family actions and policies is an essential element of passing on the faith.

2. *Seize teachable moments.* The most important times for teaching about faith cannot be programmed or planned in advance. Life gives each family many unexpected situations and experiences out of which the most important lessons of faith can be drawn. A personal experience might help to underline the importance of seizing teachable moments. I have had the most profound discussions about faith with my children when questions arise out of the context of their lives. Many years ago, Grandma and Grandpa's dog, Snoopy, became very ill. Snoopy was old and a bit feeble; the grandchildren always gave him special attention. One day Snoopy's back legs became paralyzed and he wasn't able to walk any longer. Grandma and Grandpa decided it was time to gather the grandchildren to say their last good-byes and to have Snoopy put down. It was a touching scene to witness the tenderness that was expressed among the children and Snoopy as he tried to stand on his frail

9

legs and lick their faces. Later that evening, as I was taking the children upstairs for their bedtime reading, I developed a cramp in my leg. When I grabbed my thigh and began to limp up the last few steps, our young son became alarmed. "Dad, are you going to die like Snoopy, now?" he asked. Here was a teachable moment. I seized it and had a deeper discussion about death and the afterlife than I ever thought possible with young children.

Teachable moments occur within the context of daily life. The time to talk about Jesus' law of love is not only when the curriculum requires it, but when siblings or neighbors are fighting. The time to talk about the responsibility of being church members is not merely when a child is preparing for a sacrament, but when the chores need to get done. The time to talk about the revealing symbol of water may be after a refreshing swim in a lake. The time to talk about the wonders

As models of God's love, parents need to forgive lovingly no matter what.

of creation may be when the bird's egg is found in the grass. Parents need to seize teachable moments as they arise to help children see how faith is part and parcel of their daily lives.

3. *Discipline consistently and forgive lovingly.* Through discipline, children begin to recognize the need for moral principles and ethical standards. When certain rules of conduct are enforced on a regular basis, children begin to see how guidelines need to shape their behavior. They learn that they need to think about more than themselves in making decisions. They learn that a person has responsibilities that go beyond

personal wants and even needs. To live in the human community means to respect the rights and needs of others as well as one's own. Only when discipline is applied consistently do children gradually

Parents should be able to say to their children, "Do as I do."

recognize the importance of moral guidelines. If something is wrong only sometimes, the child becomes confused about standards. Is right and wrong determined by the whim of a parent or dependent upon how an adult feels at the moment? Consistency ensures that the child gets the same message repeated again and again. This does not necessarily mean that there are no exceptions or that parents are always perfect in following through on their principles. It does mean that it is important to be as consistent as possible in applying the guidelines that should shape the characters of children.

The second aspect of this element of forming faith is to forgive lovingly. This dimension is as important as the consistent discipline. Loving forgiveness conveys the message that the child is always valued, always precious, and always lovable, and never loses dignity. Parents represent the unconditional love of God that is never withdrawn. God's love is without strings attached. There are no "ifs, ands, or buts" about God's love. God's love is not dependent on correct behavior. As models of God's love, parents need to forgive lovingly no matter what. Through this forgiveness, children will come to glimpse the amazing, ever-present, powerful force of love that is God's presence in the life of every human person.

4. *Create traditions.* For very young children, a tradition is anything the family

does more than once. Traditions include stories, rituals, special foods and actions that are repeated by a family. Traditions should express the family's values or priorities. They should become another method by which the family passes on the way of seeing that is faith. A tradition may be as simple as a special Christmas prayer (see page 129) that a family repeats year after year at their Christmas Eve dinner. It may be as extensive as a weekly "Hunger Meal" (see page 19) that a family creates throughout the six weeks of Lent every year. It might include drinking from a "Family Sharing Cup" on birthdays or other special occasions (see pages 71-88) or walking together as a family on a community's annual Hike for Hunger. With traditions that are repeated year after year, the family's faith becomes part of the rhythm of life. Traditions help the family reflect upon and celebrate its faith.

5. *Model core values.* There is nothing that speaks louder than good example or bad example. The popular adage, "Do as I say, not as I do" is a guideline for totally ineffective parenting. Parents should be able to say to their children, "Do as I do." Parental example puts flesh on parents' words and power behind their principles. If children see their parents acting upon their faith, sacrificing their time and sharing their talents and money, they will probably recognize the importance of that faith. It is important to help children see those involvements and sacrifices that are the result of faith. Whenever possible, children should accompany parents when they are involved in service activities. When Mom or Dad are at a meeting or are engaged in a project that carries out the challenge of faith, this fact should be shared with the children. Having parents share the sense of satisfaction and joy that is often derived from lending a helping hand also helps children see the importance of faith.

6. *Be a reflective family of prayer.* Too often today the hectic pace of life keeps family members apart from each other, unable to spend as much time together as they'd like. Nurturing family faith does take time. When we recognize how important this process is, we can begin to carve out the time from the busyness of

---

It is the profound vocation of parents to fashion people of faith.

---

life. Some activities or commitments may have to be sacrificed. The reflective family of prayer takes the time required. Prayer becomes a regular family activity. Some time to think about and listen to God's word is required for the genuine life of faith. Children learn to see with the eyes of faith when families express their praise and petitions to a loving God. When the family takes time to listen to God's voice, children learn to see that God is a constant and loving presence in the lives of faithful people.

It is the profound vocation of parents to fashion people of faith. The entire extended family must take upon itself the responsibility of helping children see God's presence and power in their lives. Through witness and celebration, prayer and service, discussion and tradition, the family becomes a rich soil within which the seeds of faith can blossom and bear fruit. Children come to see God's constant loving presence in the context of the family that prays together, serves together, and has fun together.

11

FAMILY ACTIVITIES

PUT IT ON THE CALENDAR

A new year gives us the chance to look at the months ahead and make some decisions about family time. Gather the family together and talk about the kinds of activities that family members enjoy most. You may wish to choose one afternoon or evening a month that will be devoted to these special family activities. If Mom likes flowers, you may want to spend one afternoon visiting an arboretum or a spring afternoon planting flowers with the whole family. If one of the children likes to roller skate, the family might spend an afternoon at the roller rink. An afternoon or evening might be spent at a baseball or basketball game, going fishing, visiting the library, seeing a play, and so on. Be careful not to stretch the family budget too thin. There are many fun activities that can be enjoyed with little or no expense. Once a family activity has been marked on the calendar, consider it a priority. Only the most serious need can take the place of the family commitment.

SERVANT CHURCH TODAY

Talk about the understanding of church as a servant in the world. Ask everyone to contribute ideas about what the church should be doing in the world. How should the church be actively providing service? What kinds of needs do people have? Give each member of the family a section of the newspaper or a recent magazine and ask them to find pictures and stories that tell of the needs of the human community. Even very young children can identify pictures of people who are in need. After about ten minutes, make a collage of pictures and words that show the kinds of needs that people are experiencing in our world. You can make a collage by pasting your pictures and words on a piece of construction paper or cardboard. After you share each other's findings, talk about how you as a family might help meet one of the needs portrayed in your collage. If you wish, post the collage in a prominent place in the house as a reminder of your call to be servants to the needy in our world.

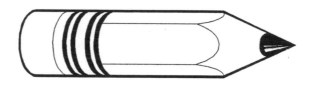

NEW YEAR'S RESOLUTIONS

Have a round-robin discussion about what changes family members would like to see in the family and in each other in the new year. All family members should have a chance to share their perspectives. Be gentle but honest with each other. Sometimes it is helpful to suggest that each person say one thing that he or she would like to see changed in another member of the family. Two suggestions for improvement can be given for the parents. After listening to the family's suggestions, each family member decides what one or two improvements he or she would like to make. These improvements should be specific concrete actions that the person can do or stop doing. You may wish to hand out slips of paper so that persons can write down the specific behaviors or actions they are planning for their improvement. This paper should be put away in a safe place. One day of the week should be assigned as the "change checker" day. On this day, each person in the family reflects on his or her New Year's resolutions to see what progress has been made.

THE WITNESS STAND

At the end of your next family meal, give everyone a chance to be on the witness stand. Everyone else in the family has an opportunity to ask the person on the witness stand a question. If you wish, you may have each person who takes the witness stand repeat the promise: "I, _____, promise to tell the truth, the whole truth and nothing but the truth." The following questions may get you thinking about how you might question the witness: What was your happiest moment today? What do you want to be when you grow up? If you could change something in the world right now, what would it be? What was the most embarrassing moment of your life?

LOVE LETTERS

Spend 30-60 minutes some evening or weekend writing love letters. Each member of the family should choose someone in the immediate or extended family to whom they wish to write a love letter. Parents may already have written a love letter to each of their children. The letter may be as simple as a listing of reasons under the heading, "I love you because...." Young children enjoy writing letters if they don't have to spell and write all the words themselves. Let the young children in the family dictate their letters to an older child or adult who will write the letter as dictated. Provide crayons or colored pencils for those who wish to decorate their letters.

CELEBRATING LOVE: VALENTINE'S DAY

TOGETHER IN LOVE

One of the most important things you can do for your family is to become involved together in some activity or project that builds the community or responds to the cries of need in our society. It makes little difference if the activity is participation in an ecology clean-up campaign, a bike-a-thon for a hospice program, a hike for the hungry, visiting shut-ins from your church community, or working at a meal program for the poor. What is important is that the family works together to put the message of Christ's love into action.

LOVE FEAST

Have a Valentine's celebration of favorite foods and good conversation. At the love feast, only compliments and positive things should be shared. Prepare family specialties or have friends bring their delicious recipes to share. Begin the meal with a brief Scripture reading from Paul's first letter to the Corinthians 13: 4-8: "Love is patient; love is kind; love is not envious or boastful or arrogant or rude. It does not insist on its own way; it is not irritable or resentful; it does not rejoice in wrongdoing, but rejoices with the truth. It bears all things, believes all things, hopes all things, endures all things. Love never ends."

Enjoy the delicious foods and good conversation. Before dessert is served, take time for everyone to compliment the person on the right. Say something about the unique talents, gifts or characteristics of this person. End the meal with a simple prayer to God in these or similar words: "Creator God, You have given us the ability to love. You have shown us how to love through Your Son, Jesus Christ. Today we celebrate Your constant loving kindness and the challenge You have given to each of us to be examples of love for one another. Help us love each other with gentleness and faithfulness. We ask this in the name of Jesus, Your Son, who lives forever and ever. Amen."

LOVE LETTER

Write a brief love letter to a member of your family. Mail it so it is received on Valentine's Day or put it in the person's lunchbox or backpack. Express some of the reasons you find this person so lovable. Mention specific talents and gifts that this individual has which enrich your family life.

LENTEN BANNERS

Create a family Lenten Banner that will remind you of the meaning of this special season of prayer and penance. Cut a piece of burlap or felt to a size of about 5" x 14" or larger if you wish. Choose a short saying for the banner, such as, "Change our hearts," "Let Us Pray," or one of your own making. Also decide on a symbol for your banner–a heart, butterfly, flower or  cross would be appropriate. With yarn, felt or textile paints, transfer your saying and symbols to the banner. Make things simple enough so that everyone in the family can join in the creative process. When the banner is finished, hang it in a prominent place.

PRETZELS: PRAYING HANDS

In the ancient Roman empire, Christians fasted from milk, eggs, butter and meat all during the Lenten season. They made small breads of the most simple ingredients–water, flour, and salt. These little breads were often shaped in the form of arms crossed in prayer. The word *pretzel* has its origin in the Latin words for "little arms." You may wish to begin a few family meals during Lent by serving a pretzel to each person as a reminder of the need for fasting and prayer. We need to fast from fighting, arguing, judging, name-calling, selfishness, and other wrongs that keep us from living out the joyful life of Jesus. We need to pray to listen to the challenge of Jesus to be a messenger of His joy and new life.

BLOSSOMS OF CARE

In the center of a large piece of poster board draw a circle 2"-3" in diameter to represent the center of a flower. Put a picture of the family in the circle. Cut out of colored construction paper 6-12 petals for each family member. As you journey through the six weeks of Lent, family members write on each of their petals the name of a good deed or act of caring that they have done. They paste their petals around the center of the flower. You may wish to do this activity once or twice a week at a special family time. As the season of Lent progresses, the flower will become a colorful blossom filled with acts of love. Acts of love might include writing a letter to a relative or friend, baking cookies for someone who is homebound, visiting someone who is lonely, saying thank you to someone whom you've taken for granted, spending ten or fifteen minutes in prayer, or helping someone with homework or another task.

LENTEN TRADITIONS

PRAYER PRETZELS

Pretzels were an important part of the early Christian's diet during Lent. Because the followers of Jesus fasted from meat, eggs, and butter during this penitential season, they made the first pretzels out of flour, water, and salt. The pretzels were shaped in the form of arms crossed in prayer. Put a bowl of pretzels in the middle of the table and gather the members of the family around the table to talk about the origin of the pretzel and what it symbolizes. Explain that prayer is talking and listening to God. In a good friendship, it is very important to spend time both talking and listening. If only one person does the talking, the relationship is out of balance. Take a moment to listen to the word of God and share with each other what that word means to us. Read Luke 11:1-13. Give everyone a chance to share his or her understanding of the passage. After everyone has shared, hold hands around the table and say the Lord's Prayer together. Have fun sharing the pretzels. You may want to continue your family night with back rubs or board games. If you wish to make a treat for Easter that carries through the image of prayer in the pretzel, cover pretzels with white chocolate which has been melted over a double boiler or in a microwave. This is a very simple treat that even young children could help make. Dip the pretzels in the melted white chocolate. Put them on wax paper to harden.

HUNGER MEAL

Set aside time on a special evening or weekend for a hunger meal. A hunger meal is a simple meal of light soup with rice or vegetables along with bread and water. There is no dessert. The meal recalls the suffering of the poor and is usually accompanied with prayer or Scripture reading and reflection. One or several family members may plan the meal. You may wish to estimate how much more it would cost to provide a regular meal and contribute this amount to the poor.

As you sit down to this simple meal, take a few minutes to reflect on the plight of the poor. You may wish to use the following verses from the Letter of James to focus your attention on the Christian challenge: "What good is it, my brothers and sisters, if you say you have faith but do not have works? Can faith save you? If a brother or sister is naked and lacks daily food, and one of you says to them, 'Go in peace; keep warm and eat your fill,' and yet you do not supply their bodily needs, what is the good of that? So faith by itself, if it has no works, is dead" (James 2:14-17).

You may want to end the meal with a prayer in these or similar words: *We thank You, Creator God, for food. Give us the courage to share what we have with those who have less. May we be sensitive to the needs of the poor. Send us Your Spirit so that we might put our faith into action. We ask this in the name of Jesus, who lives forever and ever. Amen.*

EASTER LESSONS

COLORING EASTER EGGS

If you usually color Easter eggs, this is an appropriate time to explain the symbols and meanings of Easter. Hard-boil the eggs and place them in a basket in the middle of the table. Gather the family together and explain this important symbol of Easter with these or similar words:

The egg is the oldest symbol of new life. All forms of birth and rebirth are symbolized in the egg. The egg may appear lifeless even though new life is growing inside it. Out of the egg hatches a precious new life. When we use the egg as part of our celebration of Easter, we are grateful for the gift of life, for our own lives, and for the lives of those we love. We color the eggs many pretty colors to symbolize the joy of Easter. Jesus promises us new life, so we are full of joy. The colors remind us of all the gifts God has given us. We color the eggs blue for the spring sky, green for the grass, yellow for the warm and friendly sun, red and purple and pink for the many pretty flowers.

You might wish to say the following blessing and prayer before you color the eggs: *Lord, as we enjoy coloring these Easter eggs, help us remember all the gifts of life that You have given us. We are thankful to be alive and we know that it is Your love that helps us grow. Thank You for giving us each other and for the joy You have given us in our family. Bless these eggs as a symbol of new life and bless us in the name of the Father and of the Son and of the Holy Spirit. Amen.*

EASTER EGG TREE

An Easter egg tree can be a beautiful decoration and a good reminder of the meaning of Easter as a celebration of new life. Several weeks before Easter, start blowing out eggs instead of cracking them as you use them for cooking and baking. Use a pin to poke a small hole in each end of the egg. Then, blow in one hole and force the inside of the egg out the other hole. Rinse out the empty egg shells and set them aside to color. Color your blown out eggs just as you would hard-boiled eggs. Get a small tree branch and stand it up in a pot of sand or stones. Hang the eggs on the tree branch with thread or slip the ends of the branches into the holes of the empty egg shells. You may also attach to the branches flowers made out of different colors of tissue paper or hang other symbols of Easter joy.

GROWING PROMISES

Purchase an amaryllis bulb or other bulbs that have been prepared for early blooming. Talk about the bulb as a symbol of Christ's death and resurrection. We are challenged to die with Christ, to let die bad habits and ways in which we hurt others. We are challenged to new joy and peace in our lives. Water the bulb as directed. Put the bulb in a prominent place so that the family is reminded of God's promises of new life as the green shoots and blossoms appear.

EASTER TRADITIONS

FAMILY EASTER CANDLE

During Holy Week, you may wish to create your own family Easter candle. Make or purchase a large plain white candle. Carve into the candle with a sharp knife or nutpick the cross; the alpha and omega, which are the first and last letters of Greek alphabet and symbolize that Christ is the beginning and end; and the numerals for the current year. You may wish to add the names of family members. The symbols can also be painted with acrylic paints. The candle may be lit for the first time at the Easter Vigil service on Holy Saturday evening or at the family meal on Easter. It can be the centerpiece for the family Easter dinner and should be lit for all special family occasions throughout the year. The following prayer can be used as you light the Easter candle in your home for the first time:

We ask You, Risen Lord, to be with us throughout this year with the joy of Your resurrection and new life. May our family Easter candle remind us that we share in Your glorious victory over darkness and death. May this light keep Your presence burning in our hearts so that we might be messengers of Your hope and happiness. Give us the courage, Risen Lord, to bring Your light to others by our kindness. We ask this in the name of Jesus, who lives and rules with God the Father and the Holy Spirit, one God forever and ever. Amen.

EASTER GREETINGS

One of the best ways to share our lives with others is to let them know how much we appreciate them. A few words of thanks can do a great deal to brighten another person's day. Take some time with your family to write Easter greetings to friends, grandparents, other relatives, and neighbors. Decorate your notes or letters with the symbols of Easter—butterflies, flowers, sunrise, eggs, rabbits, lambs. Be sure to thank the person to whom you are writing for the special gifts and kindness with which that person has touched your life. You may wish to send a special greeting to the various ministers in your church who serve the community in many ways.

EASTER PLACE CARDS

If you have a special Easter dinner, create a place card for each person who will be attending. An Easter design that represents the joy and life of this feast should decorate the card. You may wish to print a Scripture quotation on the reverse side of each place card.

SUMMER FUN

FAMILY GROWTH

A fun family project for the summer is planning, planting, weeding, and harvesting a garden together. Sit down with a seed catalog or visit the store together and pick out the vegetables or flowers you wish to plant in your family garden. The garden may be large or small, from an acre of land to a couple of large pots filled with good soil. Plant your seeds following the directions on the package, paying close attention to the time for planting. All the members of the family should wear their old clothes and join in the planting. Discuss with each other the miracle of life, the importance of patience, and the need for careful nourishing. We are so much like the seeds we plant—full of God's promises. We need sunshine and careful gardening to bring our gifts to fruitfulness.

MYSTERY LUNCH

With a group of friends, family members, or just someone special, plan on a lunch in the park. Each person packs a "mystery lunch" for another person. Inside the lunch must be a brief Bible passage that you would like to share with the other person. If you are doing this activity with a group, you may wish to pick names out of a hat to pair people up. Enjoy the time together and appreciate the surroundings of God's wonderful world. Before eating, give everyone a chance to read their quotation from the Bible. Bring along the baseball gloves, the badminton set, the croquet set, the knitting, or whatever else you wish. Another option is to bring books to read silently or aloud to one another.

CREATION SCAVENGER HUNT

Depending upon the ages of family members, you may wish to work in pairs, teams, or as individuals for the scavenger hunt activity. This is a great activity for inviting neighbors and friends. Each individual or team has a bag and a list of the things that they must find. In making up the list, be sure that the items are available in the area of the scavenger hunt. As people search the area and collect the items on their scavenger hunt list, they should put these into their bags. Participants are given a specified period of time, such as twenty minutes, to hunt. The person or team collecting the most items on the hunt must tell everyone how these items make him or her wonder. Suggestions for items on the scavenger hunt list are the following: pine needle, pine cone, colored stone, black stone, oak leaf, acorn, empty soda can, gum or candy wrapper, popsicle stick, berry, thorn, seed.

FAMILY ACTIVITIES
BACK TO SCHOOL NEW BEGINNINGS

TAKE NOTE

New beginnings, such as new school years, new teachers, new job challenges, new activities, often bring with them feelings of fear and apprehension. A note in a lunch box or taped to the mirror in the morning or slipped into a pocket can be a big confidence builder. One simple phrase or a special sticker can help brighten a day that is tinged with anxiety. Be creative in finding all kinds of ways of sending these messages to each other.

THE GREAT COVER-UP

Spend a night covering school books. This is a great way to recycle brown paper grocery bags. Depending upon the ages of the family members, everyone can play a role, whether it's cutting the paper, folding the width or length to fit the particular book, pulling off pieces of tape, or creating designs for the cover. As you cover each book, share ways in which each of the subject areas is important in our lives. You may end the cover-up session by asking God's blessing on these books in these or similar words: *Mother-Father God, You are the source of all knowledge, wisdom and insight. We ask You to bless these books and bless us who use them, that through them we may come to a greater understanding and reverence for Your world, each other, and You. May these tools of learning open our hearts to the mysteries of the universe and the wonders of human arts. We ask your blessing through Jesus Christ, who is with us now and promises to be with us forever. Amen.*

MANY HANDS MAKE THE WORK LIGHTER

Discuss schedules, responsibilities and each other's needs for the school year. How can we help each other have a good year? Be sure this is really a dialogue in which family members both voice their own needs and listen to the needs of others. At the end of your discussion, make a chart of jobs that each person is responsible for on each particular day of the week. Decide how you will reward yourselves for jobs well done.

BACK IN THE SADDLE AGAIN

About this time of year with all of its new beginnings, our schedules become more hectic than usual and the stresses may also mount. This is true not only for parents, of course, but also for children. It is important to take time out for rest and relaxation. If you feel comfortable with this activity, set aside a particular night when everyone will meet in the living room or family room for back rubs, foot rubs, or neck rubs— depending upon what the doctor orders.

ADVENT: PREPARING OUR HEARTS FOR CHRIST

THE LIGHT OF CHRIST

The following activity may help your family be messengers of light and peace during this Advent season. Each family member draws, on a standard 8 1/2" x 11" piece of construction paper, the outline of four candles, or glues onto it four paper candles, one for each week of Advent. Then each person cuts four flames out of yellow construction paper. Younger family members may need help with this. Explain that during Advent, the family will try to be messengers of the light and love of Christ. Tell them that as a family your light should shine so that people can see and feel the love of Jesus. Have family members think of one thing they can do throughout the first week of Advent to be messengers of light. Some suggestions are the following: helping a brother or sister with homework, doing the dishes, playing with someone new at school, spending some time in prayer each evening, listening very carefully in a class on the school subject that they dislike. Each person is to write his or her chosen action on the back of one of the yellow flames and to keep the flame in a place where it will be a reminder of the commitment. At the end of the week, each person lights that first candle by gluing the yellow flame in place. A different action should be chosen for each week of Advent. At the end of Advent, each person will have four candles aflame with good deeds that have brought light and peace into the world.

A MANGER FULL OF LOVE

This is an old custom—preparing a place for the Christ Child. All you need for this project is a manger from a creche or a small box and some straw. Each day of Advent, each family member attempts to do something special for Jesus. Helping set the table without complaining, assisting a younger child with homework, helping an older person or a neighbor with a needed chore—all would come under the heading of good deed. At the end of the day, those persons who can truthfully say that they did a special deed for Jesus today may put a piece of straw in the manger. On Christmas Eve, the Christ Child is placed on the straw. The family knows that the manger is filled with their love.

LINKS OF LOVE

Cut enough pieces of construction paper 1" x 4" so that each person in the family has two or three for each week of Advent. Each family member should be given 8-12 construction paper pieces. Throughout the week, family members try to do good deeds to prepare their hearts for Christmas. As family members accomplish their acts of kindness, they add a link to the family chain which should be hung where everyone can see it. Watch the chain of love grow as the family members work to share Christ's loving spirit with others. The chain can be hung on the Christmas tree or in a doorway to decorate your home with loving acts of kindness.

CHRISTMAS FAMILY FUN

GRATEFUL GIFTS

This is a beautiful time of the year to surprise those for whom we are especially thankful with simple gifts. Take a pint jar and cover it with a piece of cloth drawn up tightly around the sides of the container and tied at the top with a piece of colored string, ribbon, or yarn. The following are some ideas for filling the container: peanuts, homemade candy or cookies, golf balls or tees, smooth colored stones from the beach, dried flowers, and so on. Think of those special people who bring joy into your life or touch it with their talents–the mechanic, crossing guard, dance instructor, mail carrier, helpful neighbor, and so on. You may want to include a note of gratitude that tells the person how much you appreciate that person's special care.

ADVENT ANGEL

In some Christian homes, the Advent Angel visits every night or one night a week during the season of Advent. The angel leaves messages for every person in the house–just a sentence or two encouraging them to be open to Christ's presence or to use their talents to bring joy to others. Occasionally, the Advent Angel leaves a piece of candy, a tree ornament, a new pencil or a book marker. Use your imagination if you become the Advent Angel's helper.

TREE TALENTS

Gather the family together to discuss the special gifts and talents that each person has. Help family members recognize some of their important abilities. After a few minutes of this discussion, explain that, as a family, you will be making Christmas tree ornaments that express these talents and abilities. Have some or all of the following materials ready to use: posterboard, heavy-gauge wire, jar lids, markers, crayons, colored pencils, sequins, scraps of colored paper, cloth, and glue. Ornaments may be made by drawing symbols of talents on colored paper glued to the inside of jar lids. Ornaments may, for example, be musical instruments formed from wire to symbolize musical talent. They could be various shapes of the posterboard covered with sequins or scraps of material. Be creative. The important thing is to express the talents with which God has blessed each person.

SIMPLE GIFTS

Here are two ideas for simple gifts that anyone can make. For the first, you will need an orange, a small box of whole cloves, a piece of colored netting, and a ribbon or colored string. Wash and dry a fresh unpeeled orange. Push into the orange about every half inch a whole clove until the entire surface of the orange is covered with cloves. (Be sure to leave a little space between the cloves because the orange will shrink as it dries out.) Wrap the orange in the piece of colored netting and tie it with the ribbon or string. This wonderful smelling air freshener can be hung anywhere.

For the second simple gift, you will need a small jar that holds about two cups, a cup of plain instant tea mix, a half cup of instant orange breakfast drink mix, a tablespoon of cinnamon, and a fourth cup of white sugar. Combine the dry ingredients in a bowl so that they are thoroughly mixed. Put the mix into the small jar and screw on the cover. The following directions should be printed on a piece of paper and glued to the jar or lid: "Mix two rounded teaspoons with hot water, stir well, and enjoy." You may wish to decorate the jar lid or wrap the jar in a piece of brightly colored cloth tied securely at the jar's neck with a ribbon or colored string.

CHRISTMAS BANNER PROJECT

Create a family Christmas banner. Burlap or some other heavy cloth can be used for the background. Pieces of felt and other kinds of material, yarn, buttons, sequins, and pipe cleaners can be glued onto the background material to create the symbols and sayings of your Christmas message. It is important to try to include everyone's ideas on the banner or to agree on the one saying or symbol that you would like to display in your home this year. After you have discussed the meaning and design for the banner, draw the design on a piece of paper. Give everyone a chance to work on some part of the banner. Remember that the process of creating the banner is as important as how the final product looks.

VISIT OF THE WISE MEN

This activity is especially appropriate for the feast of the Epiphany, the visit of the wise men. Prepare the batter for a cake or cupcakes. Secretly put in one or two candy kisses or pieces of a chocolate bar, being sure that they are fully covered. If you wish, you may plan a special family meal celebrating the wise men's visit to the Christ Child. Other families will prefer to have a special treat time together. If you have a meal, begin with dessert. The person whose piece of cake contains the candy kiss or chunk of chocolate is the queen or king of the meal. You may wish to have a paper crown for the king or queen to wear. The king or queen gets to choose who sits where, who will do the reading or lead the prayer, what TV show the family will watch after supper, and so on. You may wish to begin the meal or treat time with the reading about the wise men from Matthew 2:1-12.

GIFTS TO LAST A LIFETIME

Have each person in the family create a collage of their talents and interests by cutting pictures, words, symbols, or phrases out of magazines or newspapers and pasting them on a paper plate or piece of construction paper. The collage should express the uniqueness of each person. Young children will need help looking for scenes or words that express their specialness. Then, give each person a chance to talk about his or her gifts, talents, and interests. You may want to give each unique creation a standing ovation.

PERSONAL CHRISTMAS GREETINGS

Set aside an afternoon or evening to create personalized Christmas cards or letters for family or friends. You may wish to make special cards with sequins, yarn, material scraps, confetti, a paper punch, and so on. Let your creative juices flow. You might print a favorite poem or even an original verse for the inside of the card. Letters are always appreciated—especially for those who are many miles away. If you are doing this activity with small children, remember that the emphasis should be on personal expression—not on how neat the final product looks.

FAMILY TALENT NIGHT

The holiday season can become so busy that family gets squeezed out of the picture. Set aside some time in your calendar for a family talent night. Be sure that everyone knows about a week in advance so that they can spend some time in preparation. Family members may wish to share a Christmas story or song, a musical piece on an instrument, a poem of their own creating or from their favorite author, a brief puppet show, a skit, a joke or two, and so on. Be creative and have fun. It might be good to set a few ground rules, such as, "No criticism is allowed" and "The person presenting gets everyone's undivided attention." End with a snack and compliments.

CHRISTMAS T-SHIRTS

Have fun creating holiday T-shirts. Purchase some acrylic paints at your local variety store. They come in tubes or plastic bottles. Many stores carry not only basic colors but neons and glitter colors as well. Each family member may work on his or her own design, or the same design might be used for the whole family, with individual names highlighted on each shirt. Most of the work for this project should be done before the paints are opened. It is important to create the design on a piece of paper first. If possible, the design should be the actual size that will be required on the T-shirt. The design should be traced lightly onto the T-shirt with a soft lead pencil. Before the paint is applied to the shirt, a piece of cardboard should be placed inside the shirt so that the paint doesn't make the front and back of the shirt stick together. Finally, allow plenty of time for the shirt to dry, following the directions on the paints.

HOUSE TO HOUSE

When you are out visiting the homes of family or friends, or out seeing the lights around town, be sure to stop in one more house on the route. Take a few minutes to stop at church for a brief quiet prayer.

FAMILY ACTIVITIES
CHRISTMAS GIVING

SPECIAL CHRISTMAS CARDS

Choose a few people to whom you would like to send homemade, personal Christmas cards. Sit down as a family for an hour some evening or weekend afternoon and create your homemade greeting cards. You may discuss suggestions for the inside message of the card. It might be a verse from the Bible or one that you create yourselves. Each family member may wish to use a different verse. Have a variety of papers and decorations available. You may wish to cut out white snow flakes and glue  them to a blue background. Cookie cutter shapes can be traced or cut out to provide other colorful decorations. You might punch holes or use a pinking shears to form a unique edge to your card. You might use sequins or glitter to add other creative touches. You can be assured that the persons who receive these cards will be delighted with the personal greetings.

CHRISTMAS I.O.U.

Along with or instead of purchasing a gift for family members or friends this Christmas, give an I.O.U. of some job or privilege that can be "cashed in" anytime during the year. Children may give their brothers or sisters an I.O.U. for two hours of playing with a special toy. An older child might give the family for whom they baby-sit an I.O.U. for two free hours of baby-sitting. Mom and Dad may extend a similar I.O.U. to friends with small children—baby-sitting for a weekend so the friends can get away. Parents may give an I.O.U. to their children for one Saturday morning breakfast at a restaurant or breakfast in bed. There are many wonderful gifts that we can give to each other. Print the I.O.U. in fancy letters. Add pictures or stickers. This is a gift of yourself.

CHRISTMAS ALL YEAR

At Christmas time, there is a flurry of activity and special programs at nursing homes, hospitals, and other institutions serving the less fortunate. At other times during the year, many lonely persons go without visitors or signs of care. During this Christmas season, reflect on your gifts as a family and the needs in your community. Then, make a commitment to get involved in some kind of service program on a regular basis throughout the year. Write out your commitment and place it in an envelope. Tuck it in the branches of your tree or lean it against the manger scene as your gift to the God of love.

FAMILY ACTIVITIES
OUR FAMILY IDENTITY

FAMILY INVESTIGATIONS

Any season is a good time to begin or continue work on your family tree. There are two versions of Jesus' family tree in the Gospels: Matthew 1:1-17 and Luke 3:23-38. Matthew wanted to show Jesus' connection to the Jewish faith, so he traced Jesus' ancestry back to Abraham, the father of Judaism. Luke, on the other hand, wanted to focus on Jesus as the universal savior—the redeemer meant for all persons. Consequently, he showed Jesus' connection to the poor and the outcast all the way back to Adam, the father of the human race. In your family investigations, go back as far as you can, listing the parents, grandparents, great grandparents, and so on. List the full name of each person, including maiden names for women. Give the date and place of birth and death for each person. Jot down stories of how and where each couple met and were married. Write on paper or record on tape any stories of important memories and events. If possible, obtain pictures of the persons on the family tree. Make copies of the family tree, stories, and pictures for each child. Even though young children will enjoy the stories and facts now, later in life they will be even more grateful for this preservation of their connectedness to the past.

FAMILY TOTEM POLES

Give each family member a small box such as a rectangular shoe box or a round oatmeal box. With paints, markers, bits of yarn and felt, construction paper, sequins, buttons, and whatever else is available, have each person make a symbol of themselves. Each family member might make the box into an animal that represents him or her. Or family members might make their own faces or a symbols of themselves. After all have completed the boxes, glue the boxes together to make a family totem pole. The youngest family member's box should be at the top. Depending upon the ages and abilities of the family members, some may need help with their part of the totem pole.

THIS IS OUR LIFE

Create a booklet that recalls the important times in the life of the family. This activity helps the family members be grateful for all the events that have brought the family to this year. There are many ways to create this booklet. It might simply be a collection of pictures that show the progress of the family through the years. It would be great if the booklet could extend back into the generations of the grandparents and great grandparents. The older children and adults in the family could even write a brief story or reflection about one of their favorite events or about one of the most important happenings in the family. Children love to hear the stories of new relationships, births, travels, new jobs, new houses, as well as sorrows and difficulties that have been part of the rich story of every family. This activity is sure to enrich every member of the family. When we recall our lives, we get in touch with how God has been powerfully present with us.

BELONGING TO THE HUMAN FAMILY

HELPING HANDS

We live in a world in which we depend on one another, even though we never see or speak with many of the people upon whom we depend. Take a few moments to think of all the people who are involved in providing a healthy breakfast: the farmer who milks the cows and grows the wheat, the dairy that purifies the milk and puts it into containers, the baker who makes the bread, the factory workers who make the cereal, the trucker who delivers the products to the store, the shelf stockers and checkout persons at the grocery store, the workers who make the toaster, the persons from the electrical company who string the electrical wires, and so on. Make a list of some of the people you most take for granted, people upon whom you depend. Take a half hour to write one or two thank-you letters to people who help you. You might write a note to the checkout person at the grocery store. You may wish to write a brief letter of appreciation to a teacher, minister, bus driver, policeman, or doctor. It may seem a little bit unusual to be writing thank-you letters to these people who are helping hands for us, but your notes of gratitude will be greatly appreciated. A thank-you is a great gift to give to another person.

NEIGHBORS ONE AND ALL

Spend an hour or several hours some week investigating with your family another culture, race, or ethnic group. There are many books in the library, from children's stories to recipe books to histories, that tell of the wonderful traditions of the peoples of the world. Plan a special family dinner with foods from the culture or group you are investigating. If you know someone from this culture, you may wish to invite the person to share some of his or her personal experiences with your family.

CREATION CLEANERS

Families, individuals, committees or groups of friends can become creation cleaners. All it takes is a trash bag and the desire to keep the world beautiful. Pick out a park, hiking trail, picnic area, beach or camp site to clean up. Take a few garbage bags and fill these with the trash that people leave lying around. You will make the world a more beautiful place for others to enjoy. After your clean-up activity, you may wish to wash up and have a family picnic lunch.

FAMILY ACTIVITIES
GIFTS OF NATURE

STAR BRIGHT

Go outside after dark to look and wonder at the stars. You may wish to take a walk hand in hand or just sit and gaze at the sky. A flashlight can be helpful in pointing out the Big Dipper, the North Star or any other constellations you may know. Libraries are full of books on the stars if you wish to do a little exploring before your actual stargazing. Watch for falling stars and make a wish. Enjoy each other's company and be thankful that God has made a whole universe of which we are one little part. God has created each one of us like each of the distant stars–unique and special.

BACKYARD BIOLOGIST

If possible, one way to become more appreciative of the wonders of creation is to look at all the marvels right under our noses. If you have a backyard, mark off an area six feet square. The area should include a bush or tree or flowers along with grass or bare soil. If you don't have a yard of your own, you might investigate a small area in a park or courtyard. You will need a magnifying glass and a notebook and pencil. The object of the investigation is to record the wonders of nature in the small area you have chosen. Be as thorough as you can. What kinds of plants do you find? What kinds of animals? What evidence do you find of creatures that may have passed over this area? If possible, try to count the number of each kind of plant and animal in your area of exploration. Find out as much as you can about the uniqueness of these animals and plants. You may want to take a trip to the library to learn more about the wonders of creation that you find. Members of the family may work together on one area or they may choose different areas and compare notes and findings after the exploration. If you wish, this kind of investigation can continue with return visits to your area after a week or a month. On the return visit you would record the changes in the area.

PICNIC IN THE PARK

Pack a picnic basket and take the family to lunch at a nearby park. Lunch doesn't have to be fancy (but it could be). Enjoy the time together as family and enjoy the surroundings of God's wonderful world. Bring along the Frisbee, the baseball gloves, or the badminton set. Another option is to bring books to read silently or to one another.

FAMILY CREATIONS

THE SHOW MUST GO ON

Plan a puppet show for the family. Make simple puppets by using markers and brown paper bags or old socks. For deluxe puppets, you may wish to sew on or glue on buttons for eyes or some yarn for hair. You can make up your own script for the show or you can use one of the children's story books. For the stage, simply turn a table on its side or make one out of a large cardboard box. It would be good for the adults also to put on part of the show, so that the children have a chance to be the audience. This way everyone has the opportunity to use personal talents and to appreciate the gifts of the other family members.

FAMILY PRAYER CLOTH

Create a family prayer cloth for your special family celebrations or prayer times. When you are finished, this cloth can be brought out whenever you are going to have an important family prayer time. First, pick out a three-foot-square piece of material in a solid color. A piece of burlap or large felt works well, although other fabrics can be used effectively. The material should be large enough so that everyone can have a section to work on at the same time. Each member of the family should create symbols or signs that indicate their particular interests and talents. It is important to draw these signs or symbols on paper first. This gives you a chance to change your mind or revise your ideas. Using sequins, glitter, yarn, cut-outs from felt or other material, pipe cleaners, acrylic paints, indelible markers, and so on, transfer your ideas to the piece of material. Smaller children will need the help of parents or older brothers and sisters. Have fun creating a family prayer cloth that will symbolize the preciousness of all the members of the family. Use your prayer cloth the next time the family has a special celebration or prayer time.

TOOTHPICK SCULPTURES

The object of this family activity is to work together to make a sculpture out of toothpicks. Depending on the size of the family, you may wish to work in one large group or several smaller groups. Give each group fifty toothpicks (unless you are really expert architects–then you get a hundred). Using glue, create whatever figure you wish. The important thing is to listen to group members' suggestions and to reach a consensus about what they wish to make. Then, be sure everyone is involved in the creation. It is best to use a rather quick-drying glue. You may wish to anchor your creations on pieces of construction paper or paper plates. You can also limit the kind of sculptures that can be made, such as circus acts, midway rides, farm machinery, the house of the future, and so on. Have fun creating together!

CREATION HOUR

Take about an hour some evening after dinner or on a weekend afternoon to be creators. You may simply have several kinds of media ready to use, such as watercolors, pencils, markers, crayons, chalk, finger paint, clay. Family members may choose to create whatever they want, using any of the media available. The purpose of this activity is not to create great works of art, but simply to let persons have fun expressing themselves. If you have young children in the family, be sure to put down lots of newspaper, dress in old clothes, and be prepared for messiness. Another way to do a creation hour is to give each family member (you may wish to work in teams, especially if  there are young children in the family) a bag filled with the same materials, such as a few buttons, pipe cleaners, paper strips, cotton balls, beans, paper rolls. Each family member or team creates something, using as many or as few of the materials as they wish. Again, the purpose of the activity is to allow family members to enjoy the creative process with each other. Be sure to give all members an opportunity to share their creations.

FAMILY COMMERCIALS

Working as individuals or in small teams, think up a new invention or product that our world needs. It could be something serious such as a cup of human kindness or a nonpolluting automobile or something silly such as a loaf of bread without crusts. Once you have decided on your invention, you need to present a commercial to sell your product. Be as creative as you can. Individuals or teams should present their commercials for the family. After the commercials have been presented, talk about some of the ways in which we can meet important needs in the world today. As a family, try to agree on one specific activity that you will do this month to be better members of the human family. You may wish to end your discussion with the following prayer:

Creator God, You have shaped us in Your own image as fellow creators. We thank You for giving us minds to think new thoughts and imaginations to dream new dreams. We thank You for giving us hands and hearts that change ideas into actions and make our dreams come true. Give us courage to use our creative powers to serve others. We ask this in Jesus' name. Amen.

FAMILY SHARING

FAMILY FUN MEAL

The object of the family fun meal is to have everyone make one specialty or favorite dish to share with the family. This activity takes a little bit of planning. Someone needs to be the coordinator of the meal, being sure that the result is a balanced and delicious family feast. To the rest of the family, the various elements of the meal might be a surprise until they are served. However, the coordinator needs to know ahead of time the kinds of dishes being prepared and the ingredients that are needed. Be sure that everyone has fun preparing the meal as well as eating it. Take time with young children to help them make something on their own. Don't worry about the mess; it'll get cleaned up soon enough. Sometimes, young children are interested in making place mats or name cards for the meal. These decorations make it a very festive occasion. Begin your special meal with a simple prayer in these or similar words: *Creator God, we thank You for the gifts and talents of each one of the members of our family. As we share this meal, we remember once again that You have called us to be a family of love and care. May we follow the example of Jesus' endless love as we cooperate with and support each other in our family. We ask this in the name of Jesus, Your Son, who lives forever and ever. Amen.*

GOOD NEWS BULLETIN BOARD

Set aside a section of the refrigerator door or put up a little bulletin board for good news only. The announcement of any accomplishment, achievement or completion of any project can be put on the good news bulletin board. Papers that show superior effort, academic excellence, or creative talent should be put on the bulletin board. Be sure to recognize what's on the bulletin board and compliment each other on the good news.

I WANT TO BE ME

Talk about hopes and dreams that family members have for occupations in the future. Dad and Mom might share how they came to work in their present occupations and how they prepared for these. If you are really industrious, it may be fun to assign family members to explore different occupations. You may even wish to set up a tour of a work place that would interest the family. By the way, has the family seen where you work? Do they understand your job?

MORE FAMILY SHARING

FAMILY BIBLE SHARING

Set aside some time for family Bible sharing. This can be done in many ways. One member of the family may be responsible for choosing a Bible passage to read and think about at the end of each meal during the week. Or you may set aside a half hour on Sunday afternoon to sit down as a family and read your favorite Bible passages to each other. However you arrange the time, give all members of the family an opportunity to pick out their favorite Bible passages. They should read their passages to the family and then give a brief explanation of the passages or why these speak to them in a special way. After your family Bible sharing, you may wish to share a tasty snack together.

SALAD SUNDAY

With all the delicious fruits and tasty vegetables of the various seasons, any time is a good time to have a "Salad Sunday." The whole family can get involved in making a special meal consisting solely of salads. Try different varieties of fruit salad, lettuce salad, vegetable salad, pasta salad. Many of these salad dishes have simple directions and can be made by young children, so that even the little ones can be involved. You may want to invite relatives or friends with the instruction that they bring a salad to share. One of the lessons of Salad Sunday is that we can keep things simple and enjoy the fruits of the earth that God has given us. You may wish to begin the meal with a prayer something like this: *Lord God, Creator of the universe, we praise You for the gifts of the earth. Thank You for delicious fruits and tasty vegetables to nourish us. Help us always to be thankful for the wonders of Your creation.*

FAMILY MURAL

Create a family mural, group painting, or collage on a large piece of posterboard, paper, or even brown paper grocery bags taped together. You may want to create a mural of your family—having each person draw a self-portrait with crayons or markers. Another possibility would be to have each member of the family draw a picture of a different family member. You might also wish to have the mural depict the beauty and wonder of creation. Each family member might take one section of the mural and cover it with his or her own views of creation. Some families like to cut pictures out of magazines to paste on their mural. Don't lose sight of the purpose, which is to enjoy creating together a reminder of the beauty of family or nature. Focus on the process of having fun together, not on the appearance of the finished product.

FAMILY ACTIVITIES
FRIENDSHIP

CELEBRATE FRIENDSHIP

Once or twice this month, invite a friend to share a meal, a movie, playtime, or a sleep-over. As you plan this activity, talk about the importance of having friends and being a friend. You may want to discuss questions such as the following: Why is it important to have friends? Who would you say is your best friend? Why? What do you think is the most important quality or characteristic of a good friend?

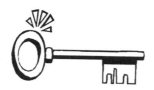

THE KEY TO FRIENDSHIP

Have each family member cut a key out of a 7" x 9" piece of construction paper. Help younger members of the family with the design and cutting out of their key. Persons should print their names at the top of their keys. The keys are then passed around to the other family members who write one quality, characteristic, or attitude that is a key to friendship for the person whose name is at the top of the keys. Try to think of traits or features that make this person a good friend. You may wish to sit at the table or in a circle. Have persons pass their keys to the right, then to the right again, and so on until everyone has had an opportunity to write on everyone else's key. When the key comes back to its owner, that person reads the friendship qualities that he or she has. If family members are old enough, you may continue this activity by having them share stories about their friends and the friendship qualities they see in their friends.

FRIENDLY FACTS

This activity is fun for children and adults alike. It is an information-gathering activity on friends. Small children will need help gathering facts. Decide on one to three friends whom you would like to get to know better. Discuss with your family a few important things you would like to know about your friends. Each person is given three sheets of paper. The person writes the name of one friend at the top of each sheet and lists down the page the kinds of information he or she would like to find out about the friend. Once this is done, each person needs to set up an interview with the friend. Younger children may wish to invite friends over to play or to have lunch or dinner. Some of the things the family members may wish to find out about their friends are the following: telephone number, address, birthday, talents, favorite color, favorite food, most exciting experience, hobbies. Members may wish to take a picture of each of their friends. After all friends have been interviewed, the family should set a date to share their friendly facts. Talk about what friends mean and why they are important in our lives.

CALLED TO BE PEACE MAKERS

PEACE RECIPES

Help small children understand what a recipe is by making something that requires following a recipe. Cookies are a good example. Set all of the ingredients for the recipe in a row on the counter or table. Talk about what each of the ingredients adds to the cookies. Then measure out the proper amounts and follow the recipe for mixing and baking instructions. After everyone knows what a recipe is, create a recipe for family peace. What are the needed ingredients and what must be done to them to make family peace? You may wish to make up a recipe for world peace, too. If children are older, you may want to create a peace recipe for a particular conflict in your community or in the world. What would a recipe for peace in the Middle East look like?

TOGETHER IN LOVE

One of the most important things you can do for your family is to become involved together in some activity or project that builds up the community or responds to the cries of need in our society. It makes little difference if the activity is participation in an ecology clean-up campaign, a bike-a-thon for a hospice program, a hike for the hungry or a meal program for the poor. What is important is that the family works together to be peacemakers in the world.

THE APPLE OF MY EYE

This is an interesting activity that helps family members become aware of the uniqueness and specialness of themselves and other elements of creation. Give each family member one apple. Explain that each person must get to know his or her apple well enough to tell it apart from other apples. However, they may not make any marks on their apples. Give them time to look at all sides of their apples. After a few minutes, collect the apples. You may want to put the apples in a bag and gently mix them up. Then put them in a basket in the middle of the table. Have family members try to pick out their apples. You may wish to ask these or similar questions as you complete this activity: How are we like apples? What makes us different from one another? What makes us alike?

READING & WRITING & WATCHING TOGETHER

NEWS HOUNDS

Gather the family together to read the newspaper. Give everyone a section. Parents, grandparents, or older brothers or sisters can read to the smaller children. After fifteen or twenty minutes of reading, give everyone an opportunity to share what they found to be most interesting or important. Many schools have current events quizzes in social studies class. Reading and sharing newspaper stories can be very helpful for students. You may find that some good discussions develop out of your sharing. You may wish to ask what good news was found. Is there any news that shows God's presence and care in the world?

WE CAN DO IT TOGETHER

The purpose of this activity is to enjoy the challenge and fun of working together as a family on a common task. Do one or several of the following activities. Everyone wins in these family activities. After all are finished, enjoy a snack together and give back rubs or foot massages or read stories to each other. Things to do together:

1. Write the letters of the alphabet down the side of an empty sheet of paper. Now write the name of an animal that begins with each of the letters.
2. Without using "un," write twenty pairs of opposites, such as "hot-cold," "wet dry." Can you write thirty pairs of opposites?
3. Create five new road signs that would make driving and walking safer.

FAMILY FILM NIGHT

Choose a film that the whole family would like to watch. Sit down and watch it together. Discuss the film, asking each person to state why he or she liked it or disliked it. Other questions that may open up some good discussion might include the following: What part of the film did you like best? Why? What would you say this film teaches? If you could change the ending, how would you change it? Why? If you could be one of the characters, which one would you be? Why? Which character do you think you are most like? Why? Would you recommend this film to another family? Why or why not? Listen carefully to the different perspectives and opinions of family members. Don't put anybody down because they feel differently than you do or interpret something in the film differently than you do.

THE FAMILY SHIELD

Work together to create a family coat of arms or shield. First, decide upon the shape of the shield. Cut it out of heavy construction paper. Draw or write on the shield some of the identifying characteristics of your family. The shield might contain the names or signatures of each of the family members. You may wish to make up a motto or saying for your family and print it on the shield. You may wish to use symbols or words to indicate an activity that the family enjoys doing together. You may wish to put a sign of your faith in Christ in the center of your shield. Each member of the family might draw a symbol for a favorite hobby. Another possibility is to use pictures or headlines cut out of magazines to glue onto the shield. Use your imagination and be sure that everyone in the family has a part to play in the creation as you make a family shield that shows your preciousness as a unique family.

FAMILY FABLE

Gather the family together at a time when everyone can be present. Turn off the TV and create your own family story. You may want to sit in a circle on the living room rug or around a table. Share the understanding of a fable before you begin the story. A fable is a story that tells a lesson or a moral. Usually, the person who concludes the story clearly states the moral of the story. This family member can simply say, "and so the moral of the story is ...." Some fables have happy endings, and some have sad endings. Some deal with animals that talk, and some deal with people and their relationships. All family fables give us a chance to listen to each other and create something together. One member of the family begins the family fable in whatever way he or she wishes. Each person then adds to the family fable as you go around the circle. Determine before you start how many times around the family circle you will go to bring the fable to conclusion and how much time each person will be expected to speak. Generally speaking, persons should not be expected to speak for more than 45 seconds to a minute, especially if some members of your family are in preschool to early elementary grades. If family members are older, the time may be increased a little. If everyone has a good time creating the first fable, go on to a second and, possibly, a third. How about "ants on a log" for a treat after the storytelling is over? This delicacy is made by filling celery stalks with peanut butter or cream cheese and putting a few raisins (the ants) on each stalk. If you prefer popcorn or crispy squares or some other favorite, go ahead and share your favorite snack.

FAMILY ACTIVITIES
FUN FAMILY FEASTS

SALAD SUNDAY

With all the delicious fruits and tasty vegetables of the various seasons, any time is a good time to have a salad Sunday. The whole family can get involved in making a special meal made up solely of salads. Try different varieties of fruit salad, lettuce salad, vegetable salad, pasta salad. Many of these salad dishes have simple directions and can be made by the children themselves.
You may want to invite relatives or friends with the instruction that they bring a salad to share. One of the lessons of Salad Sunday is that we can keep things simple and enjoy the fruits of the earth that God has given us. You may wish to begin the meal with a prayer something like this: *Lord God, Creator of the universe, we praise You for the gifts of the earth. Thank You for delicious fruits and tasty vegetables to nourish us. Help us to always be thankful for the wonders of Your creation.*

YOU ARE WHAT YOU EAT

Plan a special meal with the family in which every family member must make something new. Yes, that's right, something that you've never tried before. The world is full of cookbooks and newspaper columns with all kinds of recipes. Children of all ages can help in the preparations. You might include some ethnic dishes from around the world so that everyone learns to appreciate the many different cultures that make up our human family. Give someone the assignment of making up a simple meal prayer. Finally, enjoy each other's company and the new tastes and flavors you've experienced.

BREAD FOR THE BODY

As we reflect on the one body of which we are all members, we begin to see that we have a responsibility to the other parts of the body that we form. One interesting way of recognizing our unity is to reflect on the symbol of bread. You may wish to get three different and distinct breads that symbolize three different countries or areas of the world. French bread, Vienna bread and Russian rye are just a few of the varieties that you will find in almost any bakery. Taste the different kinds of bread and think about how the various peoples that make up our world are different and yet the same. You may wish to have a meal that is made up of dishes from various cultures. At the end of the meal, say a prayer of thanksgiving for all the different kinds of people that make up one human family.

SPEECH, SPEECH

You may like to have the family spend some time giving speeches. This is a good way of practicing not only listening but speaking and creating as well. Give everyone a chance to choose a topic and to prepare a speech on that topic. The following are some possible topics: my favorite vacation, my greatest talent, my most interesting day, the best birthday party in the world, my dreams for the future, what I would do if I had a million dollars. Depending on the age of the person speaking, you may limit the speech to one, two, or three minutes. The audience must give the speaker total and undivided attention. After the speeches, you may want to enjoy a snack together and discuss some of the creative ideas or new insights that came out of the speeches.

FAIR SHARE

Set aside one evening this month or an hour or two on a weekend for family sharing. Each member of the family will be asked to bring something to share. It could be a favorite poem, a story, a drawing, a song, an idea for an invention, a new recipe, and so on. Give everyone the opportunity to share what he or she has brought. Listen to members of the family read their stories or poems. Listen to the music they like and discuss why they like it. Listen to them explain their drawings, ideas, recipes, and so on. Have fun learning from each other and being with each other. Be sure the TV is turned off.

"ME BOOKS"

Gather the members of the family to create autobiographies or "me books." Each person should be given five or six sheets of white paper and two pieces of construction paper for the covers. Each booklet should have the following parts: A) a self-portrait, B) a page of "likes" or a listing of the person's favorite food, color, activity, sport, book, and so on, C) a drawing of the family, D) a page of family compliments or a listing of a talent or gift that the person sees in each other member of the family, and E) a "thank you" prayer. Provide crayons, colored pencils, paste and scissors, and other tools that may be helpful in the creations. Help the younger children, but allow them to do whatever they can on their own books. The creation of the booklet may take more than one session, especially with younger children whose attention span is short. After all have completed their creations, share the "me books" with each other.

COMMUNICATION

LISTENING PRACTICE

Gather the family together for some fun listening practice. You will need several baby food jars or other containers of the same size. In each jar put 6-10 pieces of one ingredient such as beans, macaroni, stones, paper clips, pennies, sand, and so on. Don't let anyone see the jars. Shake each jar and ask the family to identify what is in the jar. Another fun listening activity is to use a tape recorder to record familiar sounds. Play the tape for the family to see if they can tell what is making the sound.

A FAMILY SHARE BOOK

Start a family sharing book or a family journal. The book may be a loose-leaf folder or a soft-cover notebook or one of those fancy "write-your-own books." It should be placed in a convenient location so that anyone can jot down messages, thoughts, compliments, ideas, stories, or whatever else a member of the family wishes to share. The rules are simple: anyone can write in the book; what is written can be read and shared by others. You will be surprised to see what the family share book can do for communication. Sometimes it's difficult for us to share our feelings in spoken words. It may be easier to do this in writing. Ideas and stories, stray thoughts and suggestions—all will be captured in the family share book. These writings will also bring back memories when they are read in the future.

FEELINGS CHARADES

The game of feelings charades uses bodily gestures—but no words—to communicate a specific feeling. You will need someone to print five or six feelings on small pieces of paper. Feelings such as happy, surprised, sad, and angry are appropriate for younger children. Feelings such as embarrassed, amazed, lonely, and content are a bit more challenging for older children and adults. Very young children may not be able to act out a feeling, but they are usually very good at guessing. Each person takes a turn, picking one of the slips of paper out of a dish or hat. They must then try to communicate the feeling through gestures. The rest of the family tries to guess the feeling. You may wish to set a particular time limit, such as a minute, for each feeling word. If you wish, you may ask the person who guesses the feeling to share a personal experience of this feeling.

44

GAMES FOR ALL AGES

I KNOW NEW GAME

To play this game, you will need one deck of cards without the jokers, about 15 chips, pennies or tokens for each player, and the questions printed below.

Each player is dealt 5 cards. The players stack their 5 cards in a pile and play them in order. If a person turns over a 2-6, the person must choose a question from the 1-POINT COLUMN. If a person turns over a 7-10, the person must choose a question from the 2-POINT COLUMN. If a person turns over a jack, queen or king, the person must choose a question from the 3-POINT COLUMN. When an ace is turned over, the person may choose any question in any column and the question is worth 5 points.

Play begins with the youngest in the family and advances clockwise. If a person answers the question to the satisfaction of the rest of the players, the person collects the number of chips, tokens, or pennies that correspond to that question. THE SAME PERSON CANNOT ANSWER THE SAME QUESTION TWICE. Play continues until all persons have turned over all their cards. The person with the most chips, tokens, or pennies at the end of the game has had the most luck.

1-POINT COLUMN	2-POINT COLUMN	3-POINT COLUMN
Tell something new you learned in the last week.	Name and describe a new friend.	Sing two lines from the newest song you know.
If you were to choose a new name, what would it be? Why?	If you had to make up a new motto for your school, business, or family, what would it be?	Describe a new invention our world could really use.
Tell about a new book or story you read in the last few weeks.	If you were to choose a new pet, what would it be? Why?	Make up a new meal prayer.
If you were to choose a new place to live, where would it be? Why?	If you had to design a new car, what features would it have?	If you had to create a new dance, what would it look like?
If you were to choose a new place for a vacation, where would you go? Why?	If you had to make a new sandwich, what would it have in it?	If you had to design a new home, what would it look like?

The following games have only winners; they are noncompetitive games. The object of each of the games is simply to enjoy the activity and each other. The only rules are to be gentle with each other and to cooperate so that everyone feels like a winner.

★ TOE TO TOE ★

The whole family gathers together in a circle. One person is chosen to be the SOUND. The SOUND calls out the names of two body parts, such as right hand to left hand. Each family member responds to the SOUND by touching their right hands to someone else's left hand. The SOUND might call: head to head, left hand to right ear, right knee to left ear, right hand to left heel, nose to nose or toes to toes.

After each instruction, each person takes the body part mentioned first and gently touches it to the second body part called on another member of the family. Everyone should have the chance to be the SOUND. Remember the object of the game is for everyone to have fun and feel like a winner. Be gentle with each other.

★ FAMILY STATUES ★

Gather the family together. The object of this game will be for each family member to create a statue or sculpture and to see if the other family members can guess what it is. One of the family members is given the chance to come up with an idea for family statues, such as, wild animals, farm machinery, tools, carnival rides, farm animals, things in a kitchen, office equipment. Each player then chooses one item from the category chosen and mimics a statue to portray the item. The other members try to guess what it is. After everyone has had a chance to mimic a statue, another family member is given the chance to pick a different category for family statues. Another fun option is to have family members add sound to their "performances." A different way to play this game is to have the whole family join in the making of one statue. In this version of the game, the whole family makes one animal, carnival ride, or whatever. Be gentle and enjoy each other.

LITTLE BROWN BURRO CHRISTMAS GAME

Trace the steps of the little brown burro from Nazareth to Bethlehem. There are thirty questions that the family must answer to move the burro along with Mary and Joseph to the place where Jesus was born. One member of the family is the questioner. This person must be able to read the questions and the answers that are written at the end of the list of questions. The questioner must have 42 pennies, nickels, or dimes to give to those who are answering the questions. The questioner reads the first question. Beginning with the youngest and moving to the oldest, family members take turns trying to answer the question. The person who gets the right answer, gets one coin unless the question requires three answers. Then the person must give all three correct answers and gets three coins. This procedure is followed for all questions.

The purpose of the game is to have fun recalling not only the biblical stories of the birth of Jesus, but also some of the music and other traditions that surround this great festival. The questioner moves a coin representing the little brown burro over the map to Bethlehem. You might also use the map to teach a little biblical geography.

1. What is the name of the green plant with red berries that is popular at Christmas time?

2. What does tradition teach as the names of the three wise men?

3. Name three kinds of Christmas trees.

4. What is the feast of the three kings called?

5. What is the name of Jesus' grandmother and Mary's mother?

6. What was Joseph's occupation?

7. According to Luke's Gospel, who were the first visitors after Jesus' birth?

8. According to a popular Christmas song, how many days are there in the Christmas season?

9. Why were Mary and Joseph traveling to Bethlehem?

10. Why is the Advent wreath in the form of a circle?

11. When did good King Wenceslaus look out?

12. How many Sundays of Advent are there?

13. In the popular song, my true love gave to me how many lords a-leaping?

14. Why is Christmas celebrated on December 25?

15. Why did the Holy Family travel to Egypt after Jesus was born?

16. What were the three gifts of the wise men?

17. What saint's feast do we celebrate on December 6?

18. How did the three wise men find their way to Bethlehem?

19. Name three kinds of animals that were probably in the stable with Jesus.

20. What do the English traditionally burn at Christmas time?

21. What is the traditional drink given to carolers?

22. What did Mary and Joseph take for an offering when they presented Jesus at the temple?

23. What was the name of Mary's cousin who was also having a baby?

24. In the traditional Christmas tune, how many swans are swimming?

25. What's hung by the chimney with care?

26. Under what plant are you promised a kiss at Christmas time?

27. Name three or more biblical titles for Jesus.

28. Name three or more popular religious Christmas carols.

29. What was the name of the angel who announced to Mary that she would give birth to the child Jesus?

30. Who was the emperor of Rome when Jesus was born?

ANSWERS
1. holly; 2. Caspar, Balthasar, Melchior; 3. douglas fir, scotch pine, balsam, white pine, spruce; 4. Epiphany; 5. Anne; 6. carpenter; 7. shepherds; 8. 12; 9. to register for the census; 10. to remind us of God's unending love; 11. on the feast of Stephen; 12. four; 13. ten; 14. to replace the pagan feast of lights; 15. to escape Herod's decree to kill firstborn boys two years old and under; 16.myrrh, frankincense, gold; 17. Nicholas; 18. followed the star; 19. cows, sheep, donkeys, oxen; 20. Yule log; 21. wassail; 22. two turtle doves; 23. Elizabeth; 24. seven; 25. stockings; 26. mistletoe; 27. Root of Jesse, Son of God, Prince of Peace, Emmanuel, Messiah; 28. Away in a Manger, O Holy Night, O Come All Ye Faithful, Joy to the World, Silent Night; 29. Gabriel; 30. Caesar Augustus.

LITTLE BROWN BURRO GAME BOARD

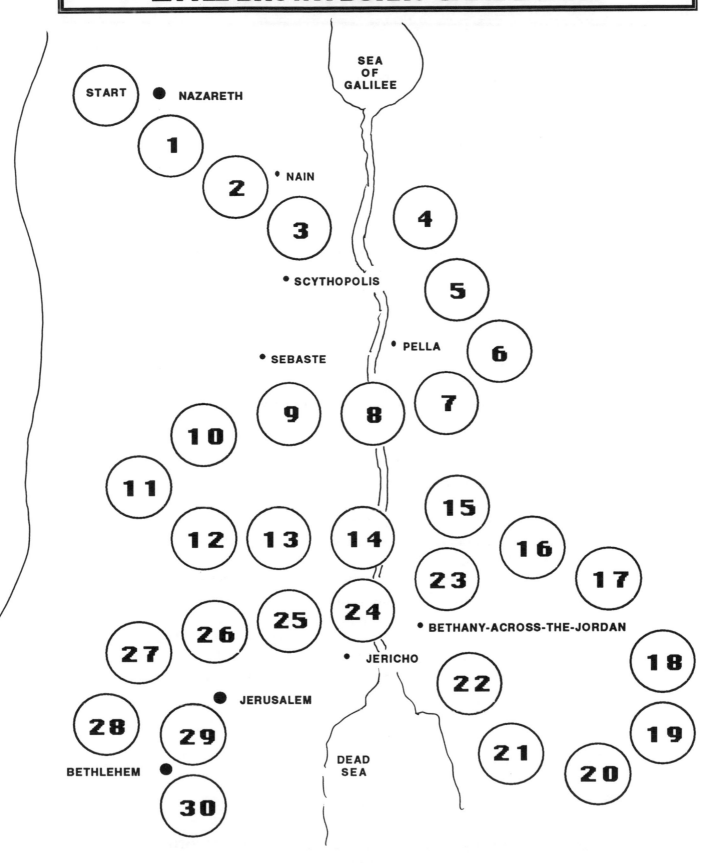

START

● NAZARETH

SEA OF GALILEE

1

2 • NAIN

3

4

• SCYTHOPOLIS

5

• SEBASTE

• PELLA

6

9 8 7

10

11

15

12 13 14 16

17

23

25 24

26 • BETHANY-ACROSS-THE-JORDAN

27 • JERICHO

22 18

JERUSALEM ●

28 29

BETHLEHEM ● DEAD SEA

21 19

20

30

©1996 Gary J. Boelhower and HI-TIME Publishing Corp. Reprinted with permission from FAMILY FAITH & FUN.

THE FAMILY TRIVIA GAME

This game can be played with the whole family; Grandma and Grandpa, aunts and uncles, too.

OBJECT: Take a revealing journey through family land. Be the first team to reach the FAMILY TRIVIA AWARDS at Finish.

BEFORE PLAY: Divide the family into 2 or 3 teams. Individuals may also play separately. Each team makes up 10 to 20 questions about themselves. The questions will be asked of the other team to see how much they know about the other members of the family. Possible questions might be: What is John's favorite color? What is Mother's favorite food? What is the date of Mom and Dad's wedding anniversary? What was Sarah's first word as a baby? What was Dad's first job? What color eyes does John have? What is Becky's favorite subject in school? Write each question on a 3" x 5" card or piece of paper. Write the answer to the question on the reverse side.

PLAY: Each team or individual chooses a coin, such as a dime, nickel or penny as a game piece to move around the board. A quarter is flipped to determine the number of spaces that a team can move. If the quarter lands on heads, the team may move 2 spaces. If the quarter lands on tails, the team may move only 1 space. All game pieces are placed on start. The team with the youngest family member begins by flipping the quarter. The team then moves 1 or 2 spaces, depending upon how the quarter landed (on heads or tails). If the team is able to answer the question addressed to it by the other team, it may move the number of spaces indicated on the square. If the team is not able to answer the question, it must stay on the square until its next turn. Teams alternate play until one team reaches FAMILY TRIVIA AWARDS.

THE FAMILY TRIVIA GAME BOARD

| START | | 3 | → | 1 | → | 1 | → | 2 |

↓ ↑ ↓

| 2 | 1 | 1 |

↓ ↑ ↓

| 1 | 2 | 2 |

↓ ↑ ↓

| 3 | 1 | 3 |

↓ ↑ ↓

| 3 | 2 | 1 |

↓ ↑ ↓

| 1 | 3 | 3 |

↓ ↑ ↓

| 1 | → | 2 | | 1 | ← | 2 |

FAMILY TRIVIA AWARDS

| 1 |
| 2 | ↑
| 1 | ↑
| 2 | ↑
| 1 | ↑
| 1 | ↑

I CAN SEE GAME

The I CAN SEE GAME is a game of descriptions, of seeing in the mind's eye. People of any age can use their own experience from which to draw descriptions of the various feelings, events, and ideas indicated in the game. Play begins with the youngest in the family and progresses to the oldest. Each player begins his or her turn by flipping two coins. If both coins land on heads, the player must follow the first direction on the list below. If both coins land on tails, the play must follow the second direction on the list. If one coin lands on heads and the other on tails, the player must follow the third direction. As each direction is followed, that number is crossed out so that the next players will not repeat previous descriptions. The first, second, and third directions from the top of the list will change as items are crossed off the list. You may continue the game as long as the items last—or you may wish to add some directions of your own.

1. Describe the time you were most embarrassed.
2. Describe your best friend.
3. Describe your favorite present.
4. Describe your favorite meal.
5. Describe your favorite dessert.
6. Describe your favorite time of day.
7. Describe your favorite season of the year.
8. Describe your favorite holiday.
9. Describe your favorite cartoon character.
10. Describe your favorite book.
11. Describe your favorite movie.
12. Describe your favorite vacation.
13. Describe silence.
14. Describe peace.
15. Describe the sensation of fear.
16. Describe the spirit of cooperation.
17. Describe the feeling of trust.
18. Describe the emotion of anger.
19. Describe the attitude of understanding.
20. Describe the outlook of acceptance.
21. Describe the way you think about God.

LISTENERS, FINDERS, KEEPERS GAME

The object of this game is to find a hidden object or treat. The difficult part is that the person who is trying to find it is blindfolded and must be guided to find it through the instructions of the rest of the family. The blindfolded family member must listen very carefully to the directions and must move cautiously. (It is best to do this in an environment where things will not get broken and where people will not get hurt.) The other family members must give clear and precise directions to help the blindfolded person find the object or treat.

One family member might wish to time the event to see if the next blindfolded person can beat the previous time. Here are the directions in sequence:

☞ Choose who will be blindfolded by picking names out of hat or choosing numbers from 1-10.

☞ Blindfold the person chosen, being sure that he or she cannot see.

☞ Someone must now silently hide an object or treat. If the blindfolded person is a young family member, the object or treat should be relatively easy to find. If the blindfolded person is older, you can increase the difficulty of finding the object or treat.

☞ After the object or treat has been hidden, other members of the family give directions to guide the blindfolded person to find it.

☞ Continue this process until everyone has had a chance to be blindfolded.

You may also wish to try the following variations on the game depending on the ages of family members. Directions can be given as opposites. In other words, if you want the blindfolded person to move to the right, you must say "left." If you wish the person to reach up, you must say "down." If you wish the person to take three steps forward, you must say "three steps backward." Another variation is to have the family members who are not blindfolded form two groups, with one group giving directions that are misleading and the other group giving directions that are correct guides to finding the object. This game increases listening skills and describing skills. It's also lots of family fun.

GAMES FOR ALL AGES
BIBLE BENDERS GAME

The object of this game is for players to learn about the Bible. Any number of persons can play. One person is appointed the librarian. This person reads the questions and confirms the answers. Play begins with the youngest person in the group and continues clockwise. There are two categories from which to choose questions: **Quotations** and **Places**. The player chooses a category.

The librarian asks a question in that category. If the player answers correctly, the rest of the group applauds. If the player does not answer correctly, the person to the right has the opportunity to give the player a clue. Persons continue to give clues until the player gives the correct answer. Once the player gives the correct answer, the person to the right of the individual who gave the last clue chooses the next question and play continues from there. If there are any questions about the correct answer, the librarian reads from the Bible the passage given for that question. The game may continue until all questions are answered correctly or until all players have had one or more chances to answer questions.

QUOTATIONS:
1. Who said, "Let the waters under the sky be gathered together into one place, and let the dry land appear"?
2. Who said, "This at last is bone of my bones and flesh of my flesh..."?
3. Who said, "You will not die; for God knows that when you eat of it your eyes will be opened..."?
4. Who said, "Will you indeed sweep away the righteous with the wicked? Suppose there are fifty righteous within the city; will you then sweep away the place and not forgive it for the fifty righteous who are in it?"
5. Who said, "Listen to this dream that I dreamed. There we were, binding sheaves in the field. Suddenly my sheaf rose and stood upright; then your sheaves gathered around it and bowed down to my sheaf"?
6. Who said, "Who am I that I should go to Pharaoh, and bring the Israelites out of Egypt?"
7. Who said, "...Where you go, I will go; Where you lodge, I will lodge; your people shall be my people, and your God my God"?
8. Who said, "I have uttered what I did not understand, things too wonderful for me, which I did not know"?
9. Who said, "For a child has been born for us, a son given to us; authority rests upon his shoulders; and he is named Wonderful Counselor, Mighty God, Everlasting Father, Prince of Peace"?
10. Who said, "I baptize you with water for repentance, but one who is more powerful than I is coming after me"?
11. Who said, "How can anyone be born after having grown old?"

12. Who said, "Sir, you have no bucket, and the well is deep. Where do you get that living water?"

13. Who said, "Lord, if you had been here, my brother would not have died"?

14. Who said, "Are you the king of the Jews?"

15. Who said, "I am no longer worthy to be called your son; treat me like one of your hired hands"?

16. Who said, "Go and search diligently for the child; and when you have found him, bring me word so that I may also go and pay him homage"?

17. Who said, "Blessed are you among women, and blessed is the fruit of your womb"?

18. Who said, "Here am I, the servant of the Lord; let it be with me according to your word"?

19. Who said, "Jesus, remember me when you come into your kingdom"?

20. Who said, "The one I will kiss is the man; arrest him"?

PLACES

1. Where did Moses receive the Ten Commandments?

2. Where was Jesus tempted by the devil?

3. Where was the wedding feast at which Jesus turned water into wine?

4. In what garden did Jesus suffer agony just before He was arrested?

5. What was the name of the hill on which Jesus was crucified?

6. What was the name of the field bought with the money Judas received for betraying Jesus?

7. The people spread their cloaks on the road as Jesus entered into what city?

8. During the census decreed by Caesar Augustus, Joseph went to the city of David which is also called what?

9. After the wise men left, an angel appeared to Joseph and told him to take the child and his mother and flee to where?

10. St. Paul's final years were spent in what city?

ANSWERS

QUOTATIONS: 1. God (Genesis 1:9) 2. Adam (Genesis 2:23) 3. serpent (Genesis 3:4) 4. Abraham (Genesis 18:23) 5. Joseph (Genesis 37:6) 6. Moses (Exodus 3:11) 7. Ruth (Ruth 1:16) 8. Job (Job 42:3) 9. Isaiah (Isaiah 9:6) 10. John the Baptist (Matthew 3:11) 11. Nicodemus (John 3:4) 12. Samaritan woman (John 4:11) 13. Martha (John 11:21) 14. Pilate (Luke 23:3) 15. prodigal son (Luke 15:18) 16. Herod (Matthew 2:8) 17. Elizabeth (Luke 1:42) 18. Mary (Luke 1:38) 19. repentant thief (Luke 23:42) 20. Judas (Matthew 26:48).

PLACES: 1. Mt. Sinai (Exodus 19:20-20:17) 2. the wilderness (Mark 1:12-13) 3. Cana of Galilee (John 2:1-12) 4. Gethsemane (Matthew 26:36) 5. Place of a Skull or Golgotha (Matthew 27:33) 6. the potter's field (Matthew 27:7) 7. Jerusalem (Mark 11:1-8) 8. Bethlehem (Luke 2:1-4) 9. Egypt (Matthew 2:13) 10. Rome (Acts 28:16).

THE THINKING CAP GAME

You will need one cap and a sheet of paper and pencil for each person playing the game. Children who cannot spell or print will need to work with an adult or older child. The object of this game is simply to remember words in a particular category that begin with particular letters. Persons take turns wearing the cap. The person wearing the cap begins the round or game by choosing a particular category or type of thing, such as, colors, vegetables, names, states, fruits, machines. Next, this person calls out the name of one item from that category. For instance, in the category of colors, the caller might call out *green*. As soon as the caller calls out the item, everyone must print this word on their paper. Then, they must try to find one other word in that category that begins with each of the letters of the original word. So, if the caller said *colors* and *green*, the players would have to try to remember other colors that begin with the letters g, r, e, e, and n. They would write these words on their sheet using the letters in the word *green* as the beginning letters of their other words. For instance, they might print *grey*, *red*, *eggshell*, *evergreen* and *nutty brown*.

If the caller chose the category of *animal* and called out *dog*, the players would have to think of an animal whose name begins with *d*, *o* and *g*; such as, donkey, oxen, and grouse. There are no winners or losers in the game. The object is simply to have fun with words and to remember some of the marvelous aspects of God's creation.

R	E	D		H	O	R	S	E
u	v	a		o	x	o	a	l
b	e	r		g	e	o	l	e
y	r	k			n	s	a	p
g	g	b				t	m	h
r	r	l				e	a	a
e	e	u				r	n	n
e	e	e					d	t
n	n						e	
							r	

TAKE MY PLACE GAME

This is a game of role-playing conflict situations. Several situations are given below. Assign roles to members of the family.

In each situation, there are two characters. In several of the situations, there is a parent and a child in conflict with each other. In these role-plays, it would be good if the parent role would be played by a child and the child role would be played by a parent. During the role-play, the family members who are in the audience should be silent and watch carefully to see how the conflict is resolved. After the resolution, the other family members can tell how they would have responded in the same situation. Family members may also wish to share their feelings about the conflict and similar experiences that they have had. Choose as many situations as you wish. If you wish, you may make up a few of your own situations and act them out.

1. Sam, who is seven years old, wants a raise in his allowance. His mother says he isn't doing his chores now, so why should he get a raise? Sam doesn't have enough money to buy some of the things that his friends have. Role-play Sam and Mom sitting down to discuss the issues. Work through the discussion until you come to a decision.

2. Sandeepa and her best friend have just broken up. Her friend lost Sandeepa's favorite tape. Sandeepa was upset that her friend could be so irresponsible. The friend didn't think a little tape was such a big deal. Sandeepa's friend calls her on the telephone to make up. Sandeepa is still upset but doesn't want to lose her friend. Talk it out until you come to a resolution.

3. Judie wanted to go to a movie with her friend. Her parents had planned a visit to her grandparents. Judie has her heart set on seeing the new movie that everyone is talking about. Judie's parents feel that family is more important. Judie and her parents sit down to solve their problem. Keep talking and sharing until you reach a solution that everyone finds agreeable.

4. Jamal talks to his friends on the telephone every night after school. He thinks this is necessary to know what his friends are up to. Sometimes his friends even help him with his homework over the phone. His older sister, Desiree, feels that she should get her share of phone time as well. Jamal and Desiree are fighting in her bedroom. Dad is fed up with their constant bickering. He tells them to sit down and figure out how to solve their problem.

5. Vanita's brother, Al, found her diary under her bed, pried open the lock and was reading it when she walked into his room. She was very angry that he would invade her privacy. He didn't think the diary was such a big deal. She didn't have any deep, dark secrets, anyway. Vanita and Al's mother asks them to talk out their problem and come to a resolution of their conflict.

THE LISTENING GAME

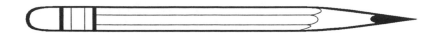

Have the family form two teams or, if family members are old enough, have them form pairs. You may want to have teams or partners sit back to back for this activity so that one person or team cannot see the other person's or team's work.

1. Each person or team creates, in the first box, an original design made up of 3-5 figures (squares, circles, triangles, lines, and/or rectangles). The design may include several of the figures listed or the same figure repeated. No more than five figures may be used in the design. **Be sure that teams or partners do not see each other's designs.**

2. After completing their designs, the teams or partners will try to draw each other's designs in the second box by following the directions they give each other. Decide which person or team will be the first to try following the other's directions. Everyone must listen very carefully and follow these rules: Do not use gestures. **Use only words. Your partner or the other team may not ask questions. Give directions only once.**

3. After the partners or teams have finished drawing the designs according to the directions given, they are to compare their drawings to the original designs. Share reflections on the difficulty of listening and understanding.

YOUR DESIGN

YOUR PARTNER'S DESIGN

SCRIPTURE CROSSWORD

Work as a family to complete this Scripture crossword puzzle. You may want to give a clue to each family member. If that person doesn't know the answer, go on to the next person, and so on. If no one can give the answer, you may all search for the answer in the Scripture reference indicated after each clue.

DOWN

1. The emperor who called the census that led Mary and Joseph to Bethlehem (Luke 2:1-7)

2. James and John are his sons (Mark 10:35-45)

3. After this person was dead for four days, Jesus called him out of the tomb (John 11:1- 44)

4. Jesus' triumphal entry into this city preceded His passion (Matthew 21:1-11)

5. The city where Jesus raised the widow's son (Luke 7:1-17)

8. The greatest in the kingdom (Matthew 18:1-7)

11. The apostle who denied that he knew Jesus (Mark 14:26-31, 66-72)

12. The apostle who betrayed Jesus (John 13:21-30)

ACROSS

4. Zechariah's son, who prepared the way for Jesus (Luke 3:1-17)

6. The garden of Jesus' agony (Mark 14:32-42)

7. The location of the wedding where Jesus revealed Himself in the sign of water made wine (John 2:1-12)

9. The city of David (Luke 2:1-7)

10. A blind man, son of Timaeus (Mark 10: 46 -52)

11. Jesus often preached against this Jewish sect and also against the scribes (Matthew 23:1-36)

12. The rich man from Arimathea who asked for Jesus' body for burial (Matthew 27:57-61)

13. To change the form or appearance of. For Jesus, this meant that His face shone like the sun and His clothes became white as light (Matthew 17:1-8)

CROSSWORD PUZZLE ANSWERS:
DOWN: 1) SUTSUGUA RASEAC 2) EEDEBEZ 3) SURAZAL 4) MELASUREJ 5) NIAN 8) NERDLIHC 11) RETEP 12) SADUJ
ACROSS: 4) NHOJ 6) ENAMESHTEG 7) ANAC 9) MEHELHTEB 10) SUEAMITRAB 11) SEESIRAHP 12) HPESOJ 13) ERUGIFSNART

GAMES FOR ALL AGES
THE FAMILY FEELINGS GAME

The purpose of the FAMILY FEELINGS game is simply to explore feelings with each other and have a fun time doing it. Good communication is at the heart of a loving family. Perhaps the hardest thing to talk about is our feelings. In fact, in our Western society we are generally not encouraged to share feelings. Consequently, many children have difficulty expressing their feelings appropriately. The FAMILY FEELINGS game is an entertaining way to become more sensitive to feelings and how they are expressed.

You will need four 1" x 2" slips of paper for each family member. To begin the game, each person takes two slips and writes a different negative feeling such as *angry*, *perplexed*, on each slip. Young children may need someone to write the feeling for them, but they will probably be able to name the feelings themselves. Then, each person takes two slips and writes a positive feeling such as *joyful*, *amazed*, on each slip.

All the slips are then placed in a bowl or cup. Starting with the oldest person, family members take turns following the procedure listed here.

✎ Pick a slip of paper from the bowl without looking at the slip. Do not show the slip to any other member of the family.

✎ Without using words, try to communicate the feeling to the other members of the family. Only gestures can be used to communicate the feeling. Again, young children may need help reading the slip, but they will probably be able to act out the feeling. You have three minutes to act out the feeling. If, after three minutes, the other members of the family have not guessed the feeling, tell them the feeling that was named on the slip.

✎ Finally, share a personal experience of this feeling. Tell the story of a time when you felt this way. What was the circumstance and who was involved? If you wish, you can do this with the happy or positive feelings only.

The game continues until every member of the family has had two chances to pick a slip and communicate a feeling.

The object of Four Fits is to find out the category into which each set fits.

The player or team must give the most specific category that would include all four items in the set. In the first set, for example, the category is "green vegetables," not just "vegetables." If a player or team identifies the category after the first clue, the player or team gets 4 points; after the second clue, 3 points; after the third clue, 2 points; after the fourth clue, 1 point. If a player or team identifies the category incorrectly after the first clue, the player loses 1 point; after the second clue, 2 points; after the third clue, 3 points; after the fourth clue, 4 points. The game can be played in many ways. The whole family can play as one, trying to get as close to a perfect score as possible. Or individuals or teams can play, keeping track of the score as they progress through the game. One person needs to be the questioner. This person also judges whether the category has been identified correctly. With younger children, more leeway needs to be given in identifying the category. You may also add your own questions. The answers to each question are given at the end of the game.

1. 1) spinach, 2) lima beans, 3) lettuce, 4) green beans
2. 1) Vermont, 2) New Hampshire, 3) Maine, 4) Rhode Island
3. 1) tulip, 2) daffodil, 3) crocus, 4) hyacinth
4. 1) pine, 2) fir, 3) blue spruce, 4) balsam
5. 1) Fresno, 2) Santa Barbara, 3) Sacramento, 4) Los Angeles
6. 1) tennis, 2) loafers, 3) wing tips, 4) high heels
7. 1) New York Times, 2) Wall Street Journal,
    3) Chicago Tribune, 4) USA Today
8. 1) peanut butter, 2) oatmeal, 3) sandwich, 4) chocolate chip
9. 1) beet, 2) carrot, 3) kolarabi, 4) turnip
10. 1) raisin, 2) cinnamon, 3) whole wheat, 4) white
11. 1) Mars, 2) Butterfinger, 3) Snickers, 4) Baby Ruth
12. 1) Pueblo, 2) Boulder, 3) Denver, 4) Colorado Springs
13. 1) math, 2) social studies, 3) reading, 4) art
14. 1) white, 2) flood, 3) spot, 4) fluorescent
15. 1) salt, 2) pepper, 3) oregano, 4) basil

16. 1) beagle, 2) collie, 3) poodle, 4) spaniel

17. 1) cinnamon, 2) Spearmint, 3) Doublemint, 4) bubble

18. 1) St. Petersburg, 2) Jacksonville, 3) Orlando, 4) Miami

19. 1) caramel, 2) cheese, 3) buttered, 4) plain

20. 1) Mars, 2) Neptune, 3) Pluto, 4) Venus

21. 1) Barbie, 2) Polly Pocket, 3) Baby-All-Gone, 4) Raggedy Ann

22. 1) oak, 2) maple, 3) elm, 4) birch

23. 1) Mark, 2) Luke, 3) Exodus, 4) Revelation

24. 1) cardinal, 2) swallow, 3) blue jay, 4) robin

25. 1) Lincoln, 2) Bush, 3) Washington, 4) Clinton

26. 1) night sounds, 2) monsters, 3) horror movies, 4) ghosts

27. 1) Springfield, 2) Worcester, 3) Cambridge, 4) Boston

28. 1) retirement, 2) Christmas, 3) surprise, 4) birthday

29. 1) Life, 2) Newsweek, 3) Ladies Home Journal, 4) Reader's Digest

30. 1) tennis, 2) squash, 3) badminton, 4) racquet ball

31. 1) drill, 2) overhead light, 3) x-ray machine, 4) toothbrushes

32. 1) basket, 2) soft, 3) base, 4) tennis

33. 1) Mark, 2) Matthew, 3) Milt, 4) Martin

34. 1) Altoona, 2) Scranton, 3) Pittsburgh, 4) Philadelphia

35. 1) football, 2) soccer, 3) baseball, 4) polo

36. 1) ketchup, 2) napkins, 3) salt, 4) sugar packets

37. 1) rose, 2) daisy, 3) tulip, 4) petunia

38. 1) mushroom, 2) vegetable, 3) chicken noodle, 4) minestrone

39. 1) drill, 2) hammer, 3) screwdriver, 4) pipe wrench

40. 1) atlas, 2) thesaurus, 3) dictionary, 4) encyclopedia

ANSWERS: 1. green vegetables 2. New England states 3. flowering spring bulbs 4. Christmas trees 5. cities in California 6. shoes 7. major newspapers 8. types of cookies 9. root vegetables 10. bread 11. candy bars 12. cities in Colorado 13. school subjects 14. lights 15. spices 16. dogs 17. gum 18. cities in Florida 19. popcorn 20. planets 21. dolls 22. trees 23. books of the Bible 24. birds 25. U.S. Presidents 26. things that scare us 27. cities in Massachusetts 28. parties 29. magazines 30. racquet sports 31. things in a dentist's office 32. balls 33. boys' names beginning with M 34. cities in Pennsylvania 35. sports played on a field 36. things found on a restaurant table 37. flowers 38. soups 39. tools 40. reference books.

BIBLE BASEBALL

Form two teams, trying to balance ages and familiarity with the Scriptures. One person will need to be the umpire, whose role will be asking the questions. (If you just can't face another baseball game this summer, have fun seeing how many correct answers you can get.) Each team should have four coins to represent base runners on the baseball field. Flip a coin to see which team is up to bat first. You may play the game by having individual team members give answers or you may choose to have the whole team try to answer each question. Decide which of these ways of playing the game you choose before you start playing.

There are two categories of questions: **Events** and **People** in the Bible. To begin play, the team that is up to bat chooses a category. Three clues are given for each answer. The umpire reads the clues. If the team gets the correct answer after the first clue, this is considered a triple and the team moves one coin to third base. A correct answer on the second clue is a double and one coin moves to second base. A correct answer after the third clue is a single and one coin moves to first base. No correct answer after the third clue brings the opposing team up to bat. A correct answer allows the team to continue play. A single advances all base runners by one base; a double advances all base runners by two bases; and a triple advances all base runners by three bases. The umpire keeps track of the runs for each team as the players come across home plate. As soon as a team fails to answer a question after the third clue, all base runners are removed from the playing field. The umpire crosses out questions as they are asked so that the same questions are not asked more than once. The game may continue until all the questions are used or for nine innings—each team being up to bat nine times.

People:

1.
   a. was a blameless person from Uz
   b. lost oxen, sheep, and children
   c. was tested by God but did not sin

2.
   a. had Uriah the Hittite killed
   b. conquered the Philistines
   c. succeeded Saul as king

3.
   a. was married to Sarah
   b. God promised him many descendants
   c. had a son, Ishmael

4.   a. was drawn out of the water
        b. had a father-in-law named Jethro
        c. God spoke to him out of a burning bush

5.   a. was a dreamer
        b. was Israel's favorite son
        c. had brothers who hated him and sold him

6.   a. was a tiller of the soil
        b. attacked and killed his brother
        c. became a restless wanderer

7.   a. adored the goddess Astarte
        b. was known for great wisdom
        c. built the temple in Jerusalem

8.   a. had seven demons driven from her
        b. thought Jesus was the gardener
        c. was one of the first persons to see the empty tomb

9.   a. didn't want Jesus to wash his feet
        b. was called *rock* by Jesus
        c. denied that he knew Jesus

10.   a. had a name that means "twin"
        b. doubted that Jesus was alive
        c. believed upon seeing Jesus

11.   a. asked Jesus about the truth
        b. was told by his wife that she had a bad dream about Jesus
        c. handed Jesus over to be crucified

12.   a. had a husband who died of sunstroke
        b. beheaded Holofernes
        c. saved the city of Bethulia

13.   a. was a Pharisee referred to as "a leader of the Jews"
        b. came to Jesus at night
        c. asked, "How can anyone be born after having grown old?"

14.   a. was an interpreter for kings
        b. read the writing on the wall
        c. was thrown into the lion's den

15.   a. was a son of Amoz
        b. said, "A child has been born for us"
        c. said, "The wolf shall live with the lamb"

16.   a. tried to flee to Tarshish
        b. spent three days and nights in the belly of a fish
        c. was called to preach to Nineveh

17. a. dipped his hand into the dish with Jesus
b. collected thirty pieces of silver
c. kissed Jesus in the garden of Gethsemane

18. a. persecuted Christians
b. had his name changed from Saul
c. was a missionary to Corinth

19. a. was a brother of Mary and Martha
b. was from Bethany
c. spent 4 days in the tomb

20. a. was a chief tax collector
b. climbed a tree to see Jesus
c. received Jesus into his home

PEOPLE ANSWERS: 1. Job (Job 1:1, 13-22) 2. David (2 Samuel 11:14-17; 1 Samuel 17:50-54; 2 Samuel 2:7) 3. Abraham (Genesis 11:29, 15:5, 16:15) 4. Moses (Exodus 2:5-10, 3:1-6) 5. Joseph (Genesis 37:3-28) 6. Cain (Genesis 4:1-12) 7. Solomon (1 Kings 11:5, 3:16-28, 6:1-37) 8. Mary Magdalene (Luke 8:2; John 20:1-18) 9. Peter (John 13:8; Matthew 16:18, 26:69-75) 10. Thomas (John 20:24-29) 11. Pilate (John 18:38; Matthew 27:19; John 19:16) 12. Judith (Judith 8:1-3, 13:4-15, 15:1-7) 13. Nicodemus (John 3:1-4) 14. Daniel (Daniel 2:24-45, 4:19-27, 5:5-28, 6:10-23) 15. Isaiah (Isaiah 1:1, 9:6, 11:6) 16. Jonah (Jonah 1:3,17; 3:1-2) 17. Judas (Matthew 26:14-25, 49) 18. Paul (Acts 8:3, 13:9, 18:1) 19. Lazarus (John 11:1-44) 20. Zacchaeus (Luke 19:1-10)

Events:
1. a. Jesus' clothes dazzling white
b. Peter, James, and John with Jesus
c. Elijah and Moses appeared

2. a. Simon of Cyrene forced to help
b. two criminals with Jesus
c. darkness fell over the whole countryside

3. a. distressing news about a man from Bethany
b. sisters, Martha and Mary, feeling great distress
c. was in a tomb for four days

4. a. forty days and nights of fasting in the wilderness
b. command to turn stones into bread
c. offer of kingdoms for worshiping the devil

5. a. freedom from slavery under Pharaoh
b. crossing through the Red Sea
c. journey led by Moses

6. a. thunder and lightning on the third day
b. God's appearance in smoke and fire
c. a call to Mount Sinai

7.   a. an important happening in the garden of Eden
   b. forbidden deed suggested by the snake
   c. eating fruit from the tree of knowledge

8.   a. Jesus on the mountainside
   b. Jesus teaching the people
   c. Jesus teaching the Beatitudes

9.   a. Jesus with the disciples near Bethany
   b. Jesus blessing the disciples with hands upraised
   c. Jesus taken up to heaven

10.   a. a noise like a strong wind heard by the disciples
    b. tongues as of fire resting on the disciples
    c. the disciples made bold in proclaiming the Gospel

11.   a. Jesus with disciples in an upstairs room
    b. during the feast of Passover
    c. Jesus taking bread and blessing it

12.   a. a shortage of wine
    b. six stone water jars needed
    c. first sign to reveal His glory

13.   a. angel appearing to a young woman in Nazareth of Galilee
    b. angel named Gabriel
    c. angel's message "The Lord is with you"

14.   a. an opening of the skies over the River Jordan
    b. the Spirit resting on Jesus
    c. John the baptizer present

15.   a. a ritual followed by Mary and Joseph
    b. first-born of Mary and Joseph brought to Jerusalem
    c. offering of two turtle doves

EVENTS ANSWERS: 1. Transfiguration (Matthew 17:1-3) 2. Crucifixion (Matthew 27:32-45) 3. Raising of Lazarus (John 11:1-44) 4. Temptation of Christ (Matthew 4:1-9) 5. Exodus (Exodus 12:31-14:30) 6. Giving of the Ten Commandments (Exodus 19:16-20:17) 7. First sin of humankind (Genesis 3:1-7) 8. Sermon on the Mount (Matthew 5:1-11) 9. Ascension (Luke 24:50-51) 10. Pentecost (Acts 2:1-33) 11. Last Supper (Mark 14:12-25) 12. Wedding feast at Cana (John 2:1-12) 13. Annunciation (Luke 1:26-28) 14. The Baptism of Jesus (Mark 1:4-11) 15. Presentation of Jesus (Luke 2:22-24)

BIBLE BASEBALL GAME BOARD

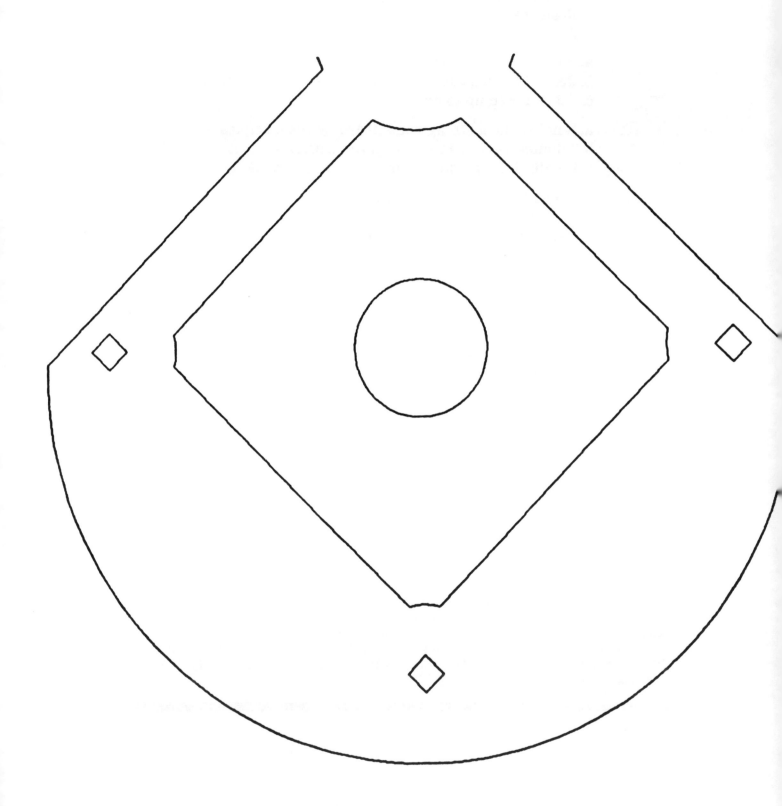

THE FAMILY SHARING CUP

THE FAMILY SHARING CUP
NEW YEAR REFLECTIONS

Choose a goblet or special cup for family sharing. Whatever the shape or size of the sharing cup, the message is the same—this is a special time of sharing, of coming together as a family to remember your love for each other and Jesus' love for each of you. A beverage enjoyed by the family should be used in the sharing cup.

Gather the family together at a special time or do this activity at the beginning or end of a family meal. Explain that you want to look at ways in which you can grow together in the coming year. What do you need to change in your lives? What can you do better? How can you follow more closely the example of Jesus?

Go around the family circle and give everyone a chance to tell what they would like to change in themselves, what they would like to improve in their own lives. Pass the family sharing cup. Each person takes a drink as all remember God's constant love for each person. Share a simple prayer that looks forward to the new year and new growth. Use these or similar words:

We praise You, Creator God, for You are a God of life. You have loved us into life and have sent Your Son, Jesus, so that we might know how to live with joy and meaning. As we look forward to the year ahead, help us change where we need changing. Help us be more loving and peace-filled people. Help us reach out to others in need. Most of all, help us know how deeply You love us. As we drink from our family sharing cup, we thank You for the marvelous gift of life and ask Your blessing on our future.

Depending upon the ages and interests of family members, you may wish to read a Bible verse or passage to add to your reflection on changes in the new year. 1 Corinthians 13:4-6 calls to mind the challenge of love that we are called to live every year.

PROMISES

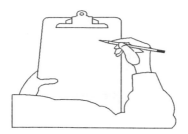

Choose a special goblet or cup to be passed around and shared to remind you of the love of Jesus and the unity of your family. The cup may be a goblet from Grandma's old set, or a pewter goblet purchased at a gift shop. Whatever the shape or size of the sharing cup, the message is the same—this is a special time of sharing, of coming together as a family to remember your love for each other and Jesus' love for each of you. Whoever is leading the prayer will be responsible for the preparations. Grape juice, chocolate milk, wine, or punch might be put into the family sharing cup, depending upon the ages and tastes of the family members.

As you gather, explain that this will be a time for reflecting on and sharing the promises and commitments in our lives. Ask everyone to share one or two examples of an important promise or commitment that they have made and how it has affected their lives. Go around the circle, giving everyone an opportunity to speak. Share a simple prayer of praise for God's promise. You may use the following prayer or your own words:

> *We praise You, Creator God, for You have loved us into existence and You are with us every moment of every day. You always keep Your promises of mercy and forgiveness. Give us Your Spirit so that we may be a loving people who keep our promises and live by Your word.*

Pass the sharing cup and, as each person drinks from the cup, ask everyone to remember God's unconditional love for that person.

Depending upon the ages and interests of family members, you may wish to read a Bible verse or passage to add to your reflection on promises. Deuteronomy 26:16-19 calls to mind the importance of our covenant with God.

THE FAMILY SHARING CUP
LENTEN JOURNEY

Choose a special goblet or cup to be passed around and shared to remind you of the love of Jesus and the unity of your family. It may be a special wine goblet from Grandma's old set, or a pewter goblet purchased at a gift shop. Whatever the shape or size of the sharing cup, the message is the same–this is a special time of sharing, of coming together as a family to remember your love for each other and Jesus' love for each of you. Whoever is leading the prayer will be responsible for the preparations. Grape juice, chocolate milk, wine, or punch might be put into the family sharing cup, depending upon the ages and tastes of the family members.

Before you pass the family sharing cup, explain that you want to think about the season of Lent and what you can do to make this a special time of Christian living. Explain that the season of Lent is a time of fasting and doing good works. During this season some people like to try to change something that needs changing in their lives. Others like to try to do extra good works to follow the example of Jesus. Allow just a few moments of silence for everyone to think about what they can do this season to follow Jesus' example and to bring greater peace and joy into the world.

Are there ways we can feed the hungry and give drink to the thirsty?
Are there ways we can shelter the homeless and visit the sick?

Now, give everyone a chance to mention one thing that they might try to do during this Lenten season to follow the example of Jesus. Share a simple prayer in these or similar words:

> *God of love, You sent Your son, Jesus, to show us the way, the truth, and the life. May we follow the example of Jesus, especially during this holy season of Lent. May we reach out our hands in service to others. May we use our voices to bring friendship and joy. May we use our minds to discover and learn. As we drink from the family sharing cup, help us realize how deeply You love each one of us. Help us understand that You are with us as we try to love as Jesus loved. Amen.*

Depending upon the ages and interests of family members, you may wish to read a Bible verse or passage to add to your Lenten reflection. Matthew 25:31-40 calls to mind how we are called to treat one another.

THE FAMILY SHARING CUP
EASTER: TRIUMPH OVER DARKNESS

Choose a special goblet or cup to be passed around for family sharing. Whatever the shape or size of the sharing cup, the message is the same—this is a special time of sharing, of coming together as a family to remember your love for each other and Jesus' love for each of you.

Whoever is leading the prayer will be responsible for the preparations. Grape juice, chocolate milk, wine, or punch might be put into the family sharing cup, depending on the ages and tastes of the family members.

Gather the family together at a special time or do this activity at the beginning or end of a family meal. Recall a time of sadness or fear. Give everyone in the family circle an opportunity to share a time when they were afraid or felt depressed or hurt. Then ask the following questions:

How did you get through this time of darkness?
Did you learn anything through this experience?

Be sure to give everyone a chance to share one response to these important questions. Pass around the family sharing cup; each person takes a drink as all remember God's constant love for each person. Share a simple prayer of hope in these or similar words:

> *Creator God, You are a God of life. You bring light out of darkness, life out of death, and joy out of sorrow. Thank You for giving us new life. Thank You for being with us and helping us through the dark times. We praise You for Your boundless love and Your constant care. As we drink from our family sharing cup, help us see again the great love that You have for each one of us.*

Depending upon the ages and interests of family members, you may wish to read a Bible verse or passage to add to your Easter reflection. John 20:11-16 calls to mind the resurrection of Christ.

EASTER NEW LIFE

Choose a special goblet or cup to be passed around for family sharing. Whatever the size or shape of the cup, the message is the same—this is a special time of sharing, of coming together as a family to remember your love for each other and God's love for you. A beverage enjoyed by the family should be used in the sharing cup.

Gather the family and explain that you wish to have a time for sharing and thinking about God's great love for all of you. Introduce the sharing time with these or similar words:

Easter is a celebration of new life, of the triumph of light over darkness and death. Let's take a few moments to think about the new life that God has created around us and in our lives.

After a few moments of silence, give everyone a chance to share examples of new life, for example, in nature, new ideas, new friendships. Then pass the sharing cup to each person. Share a prayer of Easter gratitude:

Creator of Light and Life, we praise You for the gift of new life. We thank You for new seasons, new ideas, new friendships, new signs of Your unending love. We thank You for loving us into existence and nourishing us with Your presence. We praise You in Jesus' name for being a God who is near to us, forever and ever. Amen.

Depending upon the ages and interests of family members, you may wish to read a Bible verse or passage to add to your Easter reflection. 1 Corinthians 15:20-22 calls to mind the resurrection of Christ.

Choose a special goblet or cup to be passed around for family sharing. Whatever the size or shape of the cup, the message is the same–this is a special time of sharing, of coming together as a family to remember your love for each other and God's love for you. A beverage enjoyed by the family should be used in the sharing cup.

Gather the family together at a special time or do this activity at the beginning or end of a family meal. Go around the family circle and ask everyone what they are looking forward to this summer. Ask what would they like to do as a family to make the summer ahead a time of fun and growth. You may even wish to get out the calendar and set some dates for picnics, baseball games, boat rides, museum trips, and so on. After everyone has had a chance to speak, pray a simple prayer of praise in these or similar words:

> *Creator God, You have given us life and joy. May we continue to rejoice with Your risen Son in Your gift of new life. Help us be a grateful people who see each other's love and Your love for all of us. May we be a family that listens attentively to Your word and lives out Your challenge to be of service to others. We ask this in the name of Jesus. Amen.*

Pass the family sharing cup. Each person takes a drink as all remember God's constant love for each person.

Depending upon the ages and interests of family members, you may wish to read a Bible verse or passage to add to your reflection on family summer planning. 1 Corinthians 1:10 calls to mind the need for community.

THE FAMILY SHARING CUP
SUMMER MEMORIES

The family sharing cup is a special cup or goblet filled with the favorite family beverage to be shared by all the family members. It may be a special goblet from Grandma's old set, a ceramic or wooden cup bought at an artists' fair or a pewter goblet purchased at a gift shop or jewelry store. Whatever the shape or size of the sharing cup, the message as the cup or goblet is passed to each family member is that this is a special time of sharing, of coming together as a family to remember your love for each other and Jesus' love for each person.

Set aside a special time to get out the pictures, slides, or videos of this summer's vacation, picnic, family celebration, or fun day. Remember and relive the fun days that the family had. Tell the stories again. Go around the family circle and give everyone a chance to mention the summer day or activity that they enjoyed most and for which they are most thankful. Pass the sharing cup to each person. As family members drink from the cup, ask them to think of God's love for each person and God's call for them to care for each other. Pray together a simple prayer of thanksgiving in these or similar words:

We thank You, Creator God, for all the days of summer. We praise You for the joy that we experienced in each other and in Your whole creation. We are grateful for refreshment and relaxation and for family togetherness. As we drink from our family sharing cup, help us realize how deeply You love each one of us.

Depending upon the ages and interests of family members, you may wish to read a Bible verse or passage to add to your reflection on God's gifts. Psalm 147:1, 3-5, 7-9 calls to mind some of the wonders of God's creation.

FAMILY FIRSTS

Choose a special cup or goblet to be passed around and shared to remind you of the love of Jesus and the unity of your family. It may be a special wine goblet from Grandma's old set, a ceramic or wooden cup bought at an artists' fair, or a pewter goblet purchased at a gift shop. Whatever the shape or size of the sharing cup, the message is the same–this is a special time of sharing, of coming together as family to remember your love for each other and Jesus' love for each of you.

Whoever is leading the prayer will be responsible for the preparations. Grape juice, chocolate milk, wine, or punch might be put into the family sharing cup, depending upon the ages and tastes of the family members.

Gather as a family to share family or personal "firsts." Everyone should come to this special family gathering with a "first" to share. Family members might share, for example, their first speech, their first friend, their first home run, their first goal, their first earned dollar, their first job, their first adventure, their first stitches. Go around the family circle and give each person a chance to mention at least one family or personal "first." Encourage persons to tell their own stories, and give each person your whole attention.

Pass the family sharing cup. Each person takes a drink as all remember God's constant love for each person. Say a simple prayer of thanksgiving in these or similar words:

> *Creator God, we thank You for loving us into existence. You have given us many days of newness and adventure, many moments for remembering and rejoicing. Help us be a family that believes You are walking with us in every step we take. You are with us as we continue to enjoy the "firsts" of our lives. As we drink from our family sharing cup, help us realize how deeply You love each one of us.*

Depending upon the ages and interests of family members, you may wish to read a Bible verse or passage to add to your reflection on family firsts. Philippians 1:3-6, 9-10 calls to mind the preciousness of each family member.

CHRISTMAS REMEMBERINGS

Choose a special goblet or cup for family sharing. Whatever the size or shape of the sharing cup, the message is the same–this is a special time of sharing, of coming together as a family to remember your love for each other and Jesus' love for each of you. A beverage enjoyed by the family should be used in the sharing cup.

Gather the family together at a special time or do this activity at the beginning or end of a family meal. Introduce the sharing with these or similar words:

We spend a lot of time looking forward to things–to the weekend, to graduation, to vacation, to so many things. Sometimes, it's also good for us to look back, to be thankful for the gifts that we have been given, for the good times that we have shared. What is your favorite memory of Christmas past? Can you remember a gift or happening that was special to you? Can you recall something that you will always be thankful for?

Go around the family circle and give everyone a chance to share their memories. Say a simple prayer of thanks:

Giver of all good gifts, our lives have been touched with Your love and laughter. We are thankful for the happy moments and the caring people who make up our memories. May we always remember the many ways in which You have blessed our lives during this season of light. As the years go by, may we continue to gather moments of beauty and comfort that will stay with us to give us meaning. As we drink from our family sharing cup, we thank You for the past and all of the ways in which You have been with us. We praise You for the future and all of the ways in which You will continue to journey with us. Amen.

Depending upon the ages and interests of family members, you may wish to read a Bible verse or passage to add to your reflection on Christmas rememberings. Isaiah 9:2-3, 6 calls to mind the wonder and reason for Christmas.

THE CHALLENGE OF CHRISTMAS GIVING

Choose a goblet or special cup to be used for family sharing. Whatever the size or shape of the sharing cup, the message is the same—this is a special time of sharing, of coming together as a family to remember our love for each other and Jesus' love for each of us. A beverage enjoyed by the family should be used in the sharing cup.

Gather the family together at a special time or do this activity at the beginning or end of a family meal. Explain that you want to look for ways in which you can be messengers of God's love. What can you do to be the healing hands of Jesus, the encouraging words of Jesus, the loving heart of Jesus?

Go around the family circle and give everyone a chance to share one or two ways that they can think of to put Jesus' challenge to love into practice in their lives. As you pass the family sharing cup, say a simple prayer of Christmas joy. Use these or similar words:

We praise You, loving God, for You have sent us Your Son in warm and whispered flesh. You have done the unimaginable; You have come to earth to live with us. How great must be Your love for us. How endless Your tremendous care. We rejoice in this Christmas season; in gifts, memories, and love shared with family and friends. As we drink from our family sharing cup, help us know in our hearts how deeply You love us. Help us see ways in which we can be messengers of Your love to others. We ask Your blessing upon us in the name of the Father and of the Son and of the Holy Spirit. Amen.

Depending upon the ages and interests of family members, you may wish to read a Bible verse or passage to add to your reflection on Christmas giving. Luke 4:16-19 calls to mind the responsibility to reach out to others as Jesus did.

THE FAMILY SHARING CUP
COOPERATION

Choose a special cup or goblet to be passed around for family sharing to remind you of the love of Jesus and the unity of your family. The cup may be a special wine goblet from Grandma's old set or a ceramic or wooden cup bought at an artists' fair. Whatever the shape or size of the sharing cup, the message is the same—this is a special time of sharing when you come together as family to remember your love for each other and Jesus' love for each of you.

Whoever is leading the prayer will be responsible for the preparations. Grape juice, chocolate milk, wine, or punch might be put into the sharing cup, depending upon the ages and tastes of the family members.

At the beginning or end of a family meal or at another special time, go around the family circle and ask each person to tell what *cooperation* means. Each person might also give an example of cooperation with family, friends, or neighbors. After all have had a chance to share their understanding, say a prayer for cooperation in these or similar words:

We thank You, Creator God, for making each one of us in Your image and likeness. You challenge us to be like a light set on a lampstand for all to see. Give us the courage to cooperate with others in bringing Your joy and understanding into our world. As we drink from our family sharing cup, help us realize how deeply You love each one of us and how deeply we are challenged to love each other.

Pass the family sharing cup. Each person takes a drink as all remember God's constant love for each person.

Depending upon the ages and interests of family members, you may wish to read a Bible verse or passage to add to your reflection on cooperation. 1 Corinthians 12:12-14, 27 calls to mind how all Christians are connected to each other.

THE FAMILY SHARING CUP
BIRTHDAY CELEBRATION

Choose a goblet or special cup to be used for family sharing. Fill it with the family's favorite drink. Whatever the shape or size of the sharing cup, the message is the same—this is a special time of sharing, of coming together as a family to remember your love for each other and Jesus' love for each of you.

Gather the family together at a special time or do this activity at the beginning or end of a family meal. Think about the talents, gifts, and uniqueness of the person whose birthday you are celebrating. Give everyone in the family circle an opportunity to share a compliment or a few words of praise pointing out the strengths, abilities, and uniqueness of the birthday person. Then ask the following questions:

> *What hopes and dreams do you have for the birthday person for this new year?*
> *How can we continue to be a family that loves and supports this person?*
> *How can we continue to be a family that lives out the message of Jesus?*

Again, give everyone a chance to mention one response to these important questions. Pass the family sharing cup; each person takes a drink as all remember God's constant love for each person. Pray a simple prayer of thanksgiving for the birthday person in these or similar words:

> *We thank You, Creator God, for creating _____ as a member of our loving family. Give us understanding so that we might see the preciousness of each member of our family, especially _____. Give us patience to help each other grow. Give us courage to reach out our hands to others. May we recognize _____ as a priceless gift to be cared for and loved. As we drink from our family sharing cup, help us see again the great love that You have for each one of us.*

Depending upon the ages and interests of family members, you may wish to read a Bible verse or passage to add to your reflection on this birthday. Ephesians 1:2-4 calls to mind how each of us has been blessed by God.

THE FAMILY SHARING CUP
SUCCESS STORIES

Choose a goblet or special cup to be passed around for family sharing. Fill it with the family's favorite beverage. Whatever the shape or size of the sharing cup, the message is the same–this is a special time of sharing, of coming together as a family to remember your love for each other and Jesus' love for each of you.

Gather the family together at a special time or do this activity at the beginning or end of a family meal. At your family gathering, spend some time listening closely to each other. Let each member of the family have everyone else's undivided attention–with no interruptions or negative comments. Each child and adult should share a success story–something that person or the entire family has done that the person feels good about, feels proud of. The accomplishment might be big or small, such as, "I learned how to ride my bike" or "I got a good grade on my science project" or "I broke the school record in cross-country." After each family member has shared a story, the other members may give compliments or make positive comments about the accomplishment.

Pass the sharing cup. As you drink from the cup, think of God's love for you and your call to care for each other. Pray a simple prayer of praise in these or similar words:

> *Wondrous God, You speak Your word to us in the sounds of Your creation–in roars of thunder and whispers of breezes, in the pitter-patter of raindrops, and the whine of the wind. You speak Your word to us through people, young and old, who share their wisdom or ask for help. You speak Your word to us in Your Son, Jesus Christ, who became flesh so that we could hear You more clearly. Give us the courage to listen and respond to Your word.*

Depending upon the ages and interests of family members, you may wish to read a Bible verse or passage to add to your reflection about success stories. Philippians 4:4-9 calls to mind the challenge of Christ-like living.

THE FAMILY SHARING CUP
PEACE

Choose a special cup to be passed around and shared to remind you of the love of Jesus and the unity of your family. The cup may be a special glass goblet or a ceramic cup. Whatever the shape or size of the sharing cup, the message is the same—this is a special time of sharing, of coming together as a family to remember your love for each other and Jesus' love for each of you.

Whoever is leading the prayer will be responsible for the preparations. Grape juice, chocolate milk, wine, or punch might be put into the sharing cup, depending upon the ages and tastes of the family members.

At the beginning or end of a family meal, go around the family circle and ask each person to answer these questions:

> *What does peace mean to you?*
> *How would you describe peace?*

After everyone has had a chance to share their understanding or definition, pass the family sharing cup. Each person takes a drink as all remember God's constant love for each person. Say a simple prayer of peace in these or similar words:

We thank You, Creator God, for making us peacemakers. May we bring Your peace to those who are lonely or without friends. May we bring Your peace to those who are hurting or feeling sad. May we bring Your peace to those who are angry or upset. Give us the courage to act as Your peacemakers, to love one another as brothers and sisters should. We ask this in the name of Jesus. Amen.

Depending upon the ages and interests of family members, you may wish to read a Bible verse or passage to add to your reflection on peace. Colossians 3:12-15 calls to mind the challenge of living in Christ's peace.

THE FAMILY SHARING CUP
CREATION

Choose a special cup to be passed around and shared to remind you of the love of Jesus and the unity of your family. The cup may be a special wine goblet from Grandma's old set or a ceramic or wooden cup bought at an artists' fair. Whatever the shape or size of the sharing cup, the message is the same–this is a special time of sharing, of coming together as a family to remember your love for each other and Jesus' love for each of you.

Whoever is leading the prayer will be responsible for the preparations. Grape juice, chocolate milk, wine, or punch might be put into the sharing cup, depending upon the ages and tastes of the family members.

At the beginning or end of a family meal, go around the family circle and ask everyone to tell about some part of nature for which they are grateful, perhaps an animal with which they feel a special bond or a flower that has special meaning for them. Share a simple prayer of thanksgiving in these or similar words:

We thank You, Creator God, for the world You have fashioned. We praise You for the joy we experience as we live on this earth filled with Your wonders. As we drink from our family sharing cup, help us realize how deeply You love each of us.

Depending upon the ages and interests of family members, you may wish to read a Bible verse or passage to add to your reflection on the wonders of creation. Psalm 148:1-10 calls to mind some of the mysteries of God's handiwork.

THE FAMILY SHARING CUP
FAMILY

Choose a special cup to be passed around and shared to remind you of the love of Jesus and the unity of your family. The cup may be a special wine goblet from Grandma's old set or a ceramic or wooden cup bought at an artists' fair. Whatever the size or shape of the sharing cup, the message is the same–this is a special time of sharing, of coming together as family to remember your love for each other and Jesus' love for each of you.

Whoever is leading the prayer will be responsible for the preparations. Grape juice, chocolate milk, wine, or punch might be put into the sharing cup, depending upon the ages and tastes of the family members.

At the beginning or end of a family meal, go around the family circle and ask each person to give a compliment to another member of the family. Introduce this time by focusing on the fact that God has created each person special and unique. Each of us is made in the image and likeness of God. After everyone has had a chance to compliment another family member, go around the family circle once more, giving the name of another person in the community, the larger human family, for whom they are grateful. We are also part of a larger human family. Share the name and talent or special gifts of this person. Then share a simple prayer of thanksgiving in these or similar words:

> *We thank You, God, for creating us in Your image and likeness. May we live as grateful people who recognize the great gifts that You have given us. May we never stop thanking You for the wonders of our world and the preciousness of all those who make up our human family. As we drink from our family sharing cup, help us realize how deeply You love each one of us. Amen.*

Depending upon the ages and interests of family members, you may wish to read a Bible verse or passage to add to your reflection on family unity. 1 John 4:7-9 calls to mind the preciousness of each family member.

BIBLE PRAYER SERVICES

PRAYER FOR THE BEGINNING OF LENT

This prayer may be used on Ash Wednesday or on the first Sunday of Lent as a family introduction to this holy season. You may want to provide a lighted candle, tablecloth, and cross to highlight the importance of the prayer time. You will need a leader and a reader for the prayer. Give them a chance to read their parts beforehand.

Leader: We gather together to pray at the beginning of this holy season of Lent. During this season we are challenged to look deeply at our lives to see how they match up with the life of love and sacrifice that Jesus lived. We are asked to look at the needs of our fellow human beings to see how we might live a life of love and sacrifice. We are asked to live as Jesus lived. Let us listen to one of the Gospel stories that challenges us to Christian living.

Reader: "When the Son of Man comes in his glory, and all the angels with him, then he will sit upon the throne of his glory. All the nations will be gathered before him, and he will separate people one from another as a shepherd separates the sheep from the goats, and he will put the sheep at his right hand and the goats at the left. Then the king will say to those at his right hand, 'Come, you that are blessed by my Father, inherit the kingdom prepared for you from the foundation of the world; for I was hungry and you gave me food, I was thirsty and you gave me something to drink, I was a stranger and you welcomed me, I was naked and you gave me clothing, I was sick and you took care of me, I was in prison and you visited me.' Then the righteous will answer him, 'Lord, when was it that we saw you hungry and gave you food, or thirsty and gave you something to drink? And when was it that we saw you a stranger and welcomed you, or naked and gave you clothing? And when was it that we saw you sick or in prison and visited you?' And the king will answer them, 'Truly I tell you, just as you did it to one of the least of these who are members of my family, you did it to me.'"

Matthew 25:31-40

Leader: Let us renew our baptismal promise to believe in a loving and merciful God and to act as loving and merciful sisters and brothers to one another. Please repeat after me:
I believe in one God (repeat)
I believe God has created me (repeat)
I believe in Jesus Christ (repeat) I believe Jesus loves me (repeat)
I believe in the Holy Spirit (repeat)
I believe the Spirit lives in me (repeat)

Now, each one of us will make the sign of the cross with water to remind us of our Baptism.

Leader: Creator God, You call us to follow You during this holy season of Lent, to be messengers of Your love. We promise to feed the hungry and give drink to the thirsty, to care for the sick and shelter the homeless. Give us the courage to be loving brothers and sisters to all of the members of our human family. Help us respond to their needs. We ask this in the name of Jesus who teaches us how to love now and forever. Amen.

FAMILY HUNGER MEAL PRAYER

A hunger meal is a very simple meal without dessert that recalls the suffering of the poor. It is usually accompanied with prayer, Scripture reading and reflection. One or several members of the family may plan the meal. Estimate how much more it would cost to provide a regular meal and contribute this amount to the poor. A light soup with rice and a few pieces of vegetable along with bread and water would make up the hunger meal. Before eating the meal itself, pray the following prayer and allow time for reflection. Any member of the family may lead the prayer. A leader and reader will be needed for the prayer.

Leader: We come together for this hunger meal to think about the challenge of Jesus to share our lives with others. We will eat a very simple meal tonight so that we might join our hearts with our poor sisters and brothers around the world. Let us listen to God's word calling us to be people who care for others.

Reader: " 'Come, you that are blessed by my Father, inherit the kingdom prepared for you from the foundation of the world; for I was hungry and you gave me food, I was thirsty and you gave me something to drink, I was a stranger and you welcomed me, I was naked and you gave me clothing, I was sick and you took care of me, I was in prison and you visited me.' Then the righteous will answer him, 'Lord, when was it that we saw you hungry and gave you food, or thirsty and gave you something to drink? And when was it that we saw you a stranger and welcomed you, or naked and gave you clothing? And when was it that we saw you sick or in prison and visited you?' And the king will answer them, 'Truly I tell you, just as you did it to one of the least of these who are members of my family, you did it to me.' "

Matthew 25:34-40

Leader: Especially during this Lenten season we are asked to be attentive to the needs of our brothers and sisters who are less fortunate than we are. Let us pray for the courage to respond to these needs.

All: When we see You hungry, Lord, give us the courage to share what we have. When we see You thirsty, Lord, give us the courage to give you to drink. When we see You sick or lonely or imprisoned, Lord, give us the courage to visit You, to go out of our way to care.

Leader: Very often, we do not understand how the poor are living. We forget about their needs because all of our needs have already been met. The following letter from a young person helps us understand the needs of our brothers and sisters.

Reader:

Dear hungry sisters and brothers,

    I don't know where to send this letter because you are scattered all over the world, but I just have to write it. Please try to understand that I don't know you. With my comfortable clothes, expensive tennis shoes, and a bag of munchies at my side, it's hard for me to understand what you are going through. I heard that you have to walk twenty miles or more on bare feet to carry your sick child to a clinic. I know that there are many days when you don't have any food. Your normal meal is a cup of rice and, if you're lucky, a small piece of fish twice a week. I understand that you have no house to guard you against the weather. I heard that you often feel hopeless and that you cry as you drift off to sleep dreaming of a better world.

    I know I haven't been a very good brother or sister. In fact, I'm only just beginning to understand that we all belong to the same family. I will try this Lent to share what I have with you.

Sincerely,
A member of your family

Leader: Let us pray together for our poor brothers and sisters.

All: God, Our Father, open our eyes to see the needs of our poor brothers and sisters. Open our ears so that we might hear their cry for help. As we celebrate this Lenten season of penance and prayer, open our hands in sharing. We ask this in the name of Jesus who lives forever and ever. Amen.

Serve the simple meal of soup, bread, and water. As a family, discuss what you can do to respond to the needs of the poor. You may want to start a Lenten offering cup in which you collect money for the poor. When someone gives up a candy bar or decides not to buy a soda, the money can be put into the Lenten offering cup. The family may decide to have one hunger meal a week during Lent and to contribute the cost of the regular meal to the poor.

BIBLE PRAYER SERVICES
A CELEBRATION OF FORGIVENESS

This prayer celebrates the forgiving love of God and our acceptance and understanding of one another. You may want to provide a lighted candle, tablecloth, flowers, or similar decorations that highlight the importance of the prayer time. You will need a leader and a reader for the prayer. Give them a chance to read over their part beforehand.

Leader: We gather together as a family to celebrate God's forgiving love. We come to this celebration knowing that we have hurt one another in our family and in God's larger family. Let us take a moment of quiet to be sorry for our sins.

Our response to each of our prayers is: We praise You, our forgiving God.

We praise and thank You, God, that You always forgive us. Because Your compassion and understanding have no limits, we say: We praise You, our forgiving God.

We praise and thank You, God, that You sent Your Son, Jesus, to show us how to love. Because of Your message to love even our enemies, we say: We praise You, our forgiving God.

We praise and thank You, God, for Your constant presence among us. Because You challenge us to be the best that we can be, we say: We praise You, our forgiving God.

Reader: Then Peter came and said to him, "Lord, if another member of the church sins against me, how often should I forgive? As many as seven times?" Jesus said to him, "Not seven times, but, I tell you, seventy-seven times. For this reason the kingdom of heaven may be compared to a king who wished to settle accounts with his slaves. When he began the reckoning, one who owed him ten thousand talents was brought to him; and as he could not pay, his lord ordered him to be sold, together with his wife and children and all his possessions, and payment to be made. So the slave fell on his knees before him, saying 'Have patience with me, and I will pay you everything.' And out of pity for him, the lord of that slave released him and forgave him the debt."

Matthew 18: 21-27

This is the word of the Lord: Thanks be to God.

Leader: Let us pray together:

All: God, our loving Creator, we are sorry for the times we have hurt You and each other. We know that You love us and call us to be loving to each other. Help us understand each other more. Give us eyes to see the beauty and giftedness of each member of Your human family. We ask this through Jesus Christ, who loves us today and every day. Amen.

You may wish to begin Advent with the explanation of the Advent wreath and carry this tradition of lighting candles for each week of expectation throughout the season. You can buy an Advent wreath or make one with your family. If you do not have an Advent wreath frame, simply set four candles in candle holders and surround them with a ring of greens. Gather around the Advent wreath and say the Lord's Prayer together. Explain each part of the wreath to the family.

1. The Advent wreath begins with a circle, reminding us that God's love for us has no end.

2. We put evergreens around the circle to remind us that Jesus shares His life with us every day. Evergreen branches never change their color as those of other trees do. In the same way, Jesus never changes His presence and care for us.

3. There are four candles, one for each week of Advent. We are reminded of the hundreds of years of waiting for Jesus the Savior. We also see in these candles the truth that Jesus is the light that has come into our world.

BIBLE READINGS AND PRAYERS FOR THE FOUR WEEKS OF ADVENT

As you gather around the Advent wreath each week or each day, whichever is your custom, you may wish to read the appropriate Gospel reading for that week. If the children are very young, you might choose a small portion of the reading. After the reading, give each person the opportunity to tell what message he or she found important in the reading. Others may wish to use the Advent prayer for the week as a meal prayer or evening prayer.

FIRST SUNDAY OF ADVENT
Gospel: Matthew 24:37-44
Prayer: God of life, help us stay awake and watchful for all of the ways in which you enter our lives. May we not be asleep to Your voice as it calls to us in the words of the poor. May we not be asleep to Your presence as it calls to us in the words of the poor. May we not be asleep to Your presence as it touches us in nature. May we not be asleep to Your message as it comes to us in the words of friends, parents, and fellow workers. Give us eyes to see Your care in our world. Give us ears that are attentive to Your challenging message to love others. We ask this in expectation of the coming of Your Son, Jesus Christ. Amen.

SECOND SUNDAY OF ADVENT
Gospel: Matthew 3:1-12
Prayer: God of life, may we who have been baptized with the Holy Spirit and fire reflect the warmth of Your love. May we be people of joy and hope. May we be ready to share our talents and gifts so that others might have joy. Keep us from wanting too

much when there are so many in our world who do not have the basics of life. Help us find ways to share the resources of Your earth so that all might live in peace. We ask this in expectation of the coming of Your Son, Jesus Christ. Amen.

THIRD SUNDAY OF ADVENT
Gospel: Matthew 11:2-11
Prayer: God of power and might, give us the courage to put Your word into action. Just as Jesus gave sight to the blind, may we help those who need to see Your love. May we be ready to share a friendly word, a happy smile. Just as Jesus made the deaf hear, may we speak Your word of encouragement and hope. Close our lips to criticism and open them to words of praise. Just as Jesus raised the dead, may we help those who are lonely or friendless find new life. We ask this in expectation of the coming of Your Son, Jesus Christ. Amen.

FOURTH SUNDAY OF ADVENT
Gospel: Matthew 1:18-24
Prayer: God of love, we celebrate Your presence with us. In Jesus, You have come into our history, into our human life. You are not a god who lives in the distance or stands apart from our life. Rather, You took on human flesh to experience our world, to make Your home here among us. We thank You, God, for the gift of Your Son. May we praise You throughout this holy season and throughout our lives as we see the signs of Your unending love for us. We ask this in expectation of the coming of Your Son, Jesus Christ. Amen.

CELEBRATION OF CHRISTMAS LOVE

This prayer would be appropriate for the last Sunday of Advent, Christmas eve, Christmas day, or any other special day during the Christmas season. Set the stage for your family prayer by spreading a cloth on the table and lighting a candle. A parent, grandparent, or teenager may lead the prayer. You will also need someone to be the reader. If possible, the leader and reader should prepare their parts by reading through the material at least once.

Leader: During the Christmas season we celebrate God's boundless love for us and our challenge to love one another. Let us recall the depth of God's love which was shown to us on that first Christmas night as we sing the first verse of "Silent Night."

All: Silent night, holy night. All is calm, all is bright, Round yon virgin, mother and child. Holy infant so tender and mild; Sleep in heavenly peace, sleep in heavenly peace.

Leader: Let us pray: Loving God, You have shown us the depth of Your love by sending Your Son into the world. May we be convinced of Your endless and abundant love for us. Help us share this love with all of our brothers and sisters. You challenge us to be light in the darkness, to be salt for the earth. Give us the strength to feed the hungry, to give drink to the thirsty, to clothe the naked, to shelter the homeless and to visit the sick and imprisoned. May we be messengers of Your good news today and every day. Amen.

Reader: Beloved, let us love one another, because love is from God; everyone who loves is born of God and knows God. Whoever does not love does not know God, for God is love. God's love was revealed among us in this way: God sent his only Son into the world so that we might live through him. In this is love: not that we have loved God, but that he loved us and sent his Son to be the atoning sacrifice for our sins. Beloved, since God loved us so much, we also ought to love one another.

1 John 4:7-11

Leader: Our response to God's word will be "Lord, help us love one another."

Leader: Help us understand that people everywhere belong to one family of God, we pray:

All: Lord, help us love one another.

Leader: Help us hear and respond to the needs of the poor and the oppressed in our world, we pray:

All: Lord, help us love one another.

Leader: Give us the courage to be peacemakers in our families, with our friends, and in our places of work and study, we pray:

All: Lord, help us love one another.

Leader: Help us be a Christmas people who see Your powerful presence in our world and share the gifts You have given us, we pray:

All: Lord, help us love one another.

Leader: Lord Jesus, may the peace and love of this Christmas season remain alive in our hearts throughout the year. May we take up Your challenge to put Your love into action. May we be Your hands outstretched to those in need. May we be Your voice of encouragement and comfort. Lord, give us the courage to love as You have loved today and everyday. Amen.

Leader: Let us end our prayer time together by holding hands and saying the Lord's Prayer.

All: Our Father...

BIBLE PRAYER SERVICES
A CHRISTMAS PRAYER

This prayer may be used as a meal prayer or as a special evening prayer on the last Sunday of Advent, on Christmas Eve, Christmas Day, or any other day that you gather to celebrate Christ our Light. A leader and reader will be needed for the prayer. The leader begins the service by lighting a large candle.

Leader: As we gather together, we light this candle as a symbol of Christ's light among us. It is impossible to see in the dark. When it is dark, we stumble and we are afraid. When it is light, we can see clearly. We have no need for fear, and we can see where to go. Let us be thankful for God's gift of Light, Jesus Christ, as we listen to the words of the prophet Isaiah.

Reader:
The people who walked in darkness
    have seen a great light;
those who lived in a land of deep darkness—
    on them light has shined.
You have multiplied the nation
    you have increased its joy;
they rejoice before You
    as with joy at the harvest...
For a child has been born for us,
    a son given to us;
authority rests on his shoulders;
    and he is named
Wonderful Counselor, Mighty God,
    Everlasting Father, Prince of Peace.
His authority shall grow continually,
    and there shall be endless peace
for the throne of David and his kingdom.
    He will establish and uphold it
with justice and with righteousness
from this time onward and forevermore.
Isaiah 9:2-3, 6-9

Leader: God sent Jesus into the world to bring light and peace. Jesus challenges us as His disciples to do the same. Let us ask for His guidance and wisdom as we face the challenge to be a light for others.

Leader: Lord of Light, shower us with Your Spirit that we might understand how we can best use our talents and gifts to bring Your light into the world, we pray:

All: Hear us, Prince of Peace.

Leader: Lord of Light, strengthen us with Your courage that we might take the risk to respond to those who are in need of food, shelter, comfort and care, we pray:

All: Hear us, Prince of Peace.

Leader: Lord of Light, open our ears to Your word that we might continually be challenged by Your message and example, we pray:

All: Hear us, Prince of Peace.

Leader: Lord of Light, inflame our hearts with the fire of Your love that we might always be sensitive to the voices of the poor and the oppressed in our world, we pray:

All: Hear us, Prince of Peace.

Leader: Let us pray together as children of light, asking God to come into our hearts at this Christmas season.

All: God of Light, You have chosen to be at home in our world, to be a God who is close to us. We ask You to enlighten our minds and inflame our hearts with Your love. May we have the courage to let our light shine, to reach out to others with Your compassion and forgiveness. We ask this in the name of Jesus, who lives forever and ever. Amen.

If you wish, you may end your prayer with the familiar song "This Little Light of Mine."

This little light of mine, I'm gonna let it shine.
This little light of mine, I'm gonna let it shine.
This little light of mine, I'm gonna let it shine.
Let it shine, let it shine, let it shine.

'Round the Christmas tree, I'm gonna let it shine.
'Round the Christmas tree, I'm gonna let it shine.
'Round the Christmas tree, I'm gonna let it shine.
Let it shine, let it shine, let it shine.

A PRAYER ABOUT GIVING

This prayer may be used for meal prayer or a special evening prayer on any day that you wish to celebrate your giftedness to each other. Any member of the family may lead the prayer and all should try to participate in the ritual as much as possible. (A leader and reader will be needed for the prayer.)

Leader: We gather together in prayer to celebrate how each of us is a gift to our family, how each of us adds an important contribution to our home. As we listen to the following reading, let us think about the times when we have shared gifts of care and understanding with each other.

Reader: A reading from Paul's letter to the Colossians:
As God's chosen ones, holy and beloved, clothe yourselves with compassion, kindness, humility, meekness, and patience. Bear with one another and, if anyone has a complaint against another, forgive each other; just as the Lord has forgiven you, so you also must forgive. Above all, clothe yourselves with love, which binds everything together in perfect harmony. And let the peace of Christ rule in your hearts, to which indeed you were called into one body. And be thankful.

Colossians 3:12-15

This is the word of the Lord: Thanks be to God.

Leader: Each of us is a gift to our family. Let us be grateful for the many ways in which we have received love and care from each other. And let us express our thankfulness by mentioning the gifts that others have brought into our lives. We will each take a turn to say thank you to family members for their gifts of self. (Example: Thank you, Jim, for your happy smile every morning when you come down for breakfast. OR Thanks, Dad, for the backrubs you give me at bedtime.)

Take time now to express your thankfulness.

Leader: Let us pray together in gratitude:

All: God, You are a loving God. We see Your love in the world that surrounds us, in the people who fill our lives and in the depths of our own hearts. We see Your love especially in Your Son, Jesus.

Thank You for Your gift to us. Give us the courage and will to make our lives a gift to You. Help us be kind, gentle, peaceful, and loving so that we might be gifts of care to each other and to our world. We ask this in the name of Jesus, Your Son and our brother forever. Amen.

This prayer is appropriate for any time you wish to reflect on the importance of work, such as Labor Day. Set the stage for your family prayer by spreading a cloth on the table and lighting a candle. A parent, grandparent, or teenager may lead the prayer. You will also need someone to be the reader. If possible, the leader and reader should prepare their parts by reading through the material at least once.

Leader: We gather together to think about all those people who day in and day out do their jobs with dedication and care. Let us thank God for all those people who serve our needs in so many ways.

Our response to each of our prayers is: We thank You, Lord.

Leader: For farmers who grow their crops so that others might have life and enjoy the flavors of God's many vegetables and fruits, we pray:

All: We thank You, Lord.

Leader: For bakers who rise early to mix the yeast and dough so that we might have our daily bread to satisfy our everyday hunger, we pray:

All: We thank You, Lord.

Leader: For architects, engineers, plumbers, electricians, carpenters, and all those who plan and build our homes, hospitals, schools, gymnasiums, theaters, and stores, so that we might have space in which to live and work and play, we pray:

All: We thank You, Lord.

Leader: For the leaders of our church and our country, that the Lord will fill them with wisdom and insight so that they may lead us to greater peace, deeper harmony and more generous sharing of our lives, we pray:

All: We thank You, Lord.

Reader: Now there are varieties of gifts but the same Spirit; and there are varieties of services, but the same Lord; and there are varieties of activities, but it is the same God who activates all of them in everyone. To each is given the manifestation of the Spirit for the common good.

For just as the body is one and has many members, and all the members of the body, though many, are one body, so it is with Christ. For in the one Spirit we were all baptized into one body—Jews or Greeks, slaves or free—and we were all made to drink of one Spirit.

Now you are the body of Christ and individually members of it.

1 Corinthians 12:4-7, 12-13, 27

Leader: Let us pray together:

All: Our loving God, we thank You for this celebration of our labors. Help each of us do our work in such a way that it will serve You and give honor to Your name. We ask this through Jesus Christ, who is with us today and every day. Amen.

PRAYER OF THANKS FOR NATURE

This prayer can be used any time to focus on the wonder of God's creation and to express our gratitude for all that we have received. A parent, grandparent, or teenager may lead the prayer. Prepare a space for prayer. A tablecloth, Bible, candle, or flowers can show reverence and invite a spirit of reflection. If possible, have persons prepare the parts of Leader and Reader beforehand. If this service is done with small children, you may wish to shorten the Gospel reading or tell it in your own words.

Leader: The painter pays close attention to every brush stroke and every shade of color—knowing that the painting shows to others what is in the painter's very soul. The poet chooses just the right word with just the right meaning—knowing that the creation shows to others the poet's very self. And so it is with God. The beautiful lines of the oak leaf, the colors of strawberries and tulips, carrots and dandelions, show us a beautiful God. But, even more, the first steps of a child, the first faltering words, the first question reveals a marvelous Maker. God has created a wonderful world. We see God's love in every part of the universe. Our response to each of our prayers is: Thank You, Creator God.

Leader: For fragile flowers and frosty snowflakes that show us Your gentle spirit and Your challenge of peace,

All: Thank You, Creator God.

Leader: For the red-breasted robin and the buzzing bee that show us Your constant care for all creation,

All: Thank You, Creator God.

Leader: For the golden sunrise and the refreshing breeze that give us hope,

All: Thank You, Creator God.

Leader: For clear water and delicious food that give us energy and the power to keep living and loving,

All: Thank You, Creator God.

Leader: Sometimes, in the middle of a busy day, a single rose will stop us in our tracks or a sunset will silence our talking. We may be struck with wonder at the simple, magnificent beauty that we often take for granted. At these moments we understand again how God is with us constantly in the wonders of creation. It is this attitude of wonder and awe and that the Book of Psalms shows us.

Reader: Sun and moon, praise God, praise God above all forever. Stars of heaven, praise God, praise God above all forever. Rain and frost, fire and heat, ice and snow, praise God, praise God above all forever. Light and darkness, day and night, praise God, praise God above all forever. Mountains and valleys, oceans and rivers, forests and plains, praise God, praise God above all forever. Wild beasts and tame, birds of the air, fish of the sea, praise God, praise God above all forever. Young people and old, women and men, all the family of earth, praise God, praise God above all forever.

Based on Psalm 148

Leader: Let us pray together:

All: Creator God, we praise and thank You for the wonders of creation. You show us Your constant love with the rising of the sun on each new day. You give us food, water, and air to keep us alive. You give us a world full of beauty and challenge us to care for it. You give us each other and challenge us to love. May we give You honor and glory in the care and love we show for our world and for one another. We ask this in the name of Jesus Christ who is with us today and every day. Amen.

PRAYER OF HOPE AND PEACE

Set the stage for your family prayer by spreading a cloth on the table and lighting a candle. A parent, grandparent, or teenager may lead the prayer. You will also need someone to be the reader. If possible, the leader and reader should prepare for their parts by reading through the material at least once.

Leader: God has promised us that there will be a time of perfect peace and perfect justice. God has also challenged us to work for peace and justice right now in our world. We gather together today to pray for a deeper understanding of God's vision. What would the world look like if there were perfect peace? How would people act toward each other if there were perfect justice? God challenges us to dream dreams, to have a vision of the possible, so that we have a goal to guide our Christian action. Our response to each of our prayers will be: Give us Your vision, Lord.

When we see the poor and oppressed in our world, help us recognize their tremendous worth and reach out with Your love, we pray: Give us Your vision, Lord.

When we see those who are suffering or dying, help us have faith in the resurrection and eternal life, we pray: Give us Your vision, Lord.

When we see arguing and fighting, help us believe in peace and healing, we pray: Give us Your vision, Lord.

When we see people who are lonely or afraid, help us welcome them into Your community of love, we pray: Give us Your vision, Lord.

Reader:
The wolf shall live with the lamb,
    the leopard shall lie down with the kid,
the calf and the lion and the fatling together,
    and a little child shall lead them.
The cow and the bear shall graze,
    their young shall lie down together;
    and the lion shall eat straw like the ox.
The nursing child shall play over the hole of the asp,
and the weaned child put its hand on the adder's den.
They will not hurt or destroy on all my holy mountain;
for the earth will be full of the knowledge of the Lord,
as the waters cover the sea.

Isaiah 11: 6-9

This is the word of the Lord: Thanks be to God.

Spend a few moments discussing this passage from the prophet Isaiah. What pictures come into your mind as you hear this passage? How is this passage a vision of God's justice and peace? If you were to picture God's justice and peace in our world today, how would you picture it? What images, pictures, scenes come to mind? (If you wish, members of the family may draw their pictures of God's perfect justice and peace in the world.) How can we help bring about greater justice and peace in our world today?

Leader: Let us pray together:

All: Our loving God, You are a God of great possibilities. You challenge us to believe in a world of perfect justice and peace. You tell us to hope in the future and to look forward to Your kingdom. Give us the courage to dream new dreams. Give us the insight to share Your vision of the possible. May our words and actions be a reflection of Your peace and ever-constant love. We ask this through Jesus Christ, who is with us today and every day. Amen.

RENEWAL OF BAPTISMAL PROMISES

Prepare a space for prayer. A tablecloth, Bible, candle, or flowers can show reverence and invite a spirit of reflection. If possible, have persons prepare the parts of Leader and Reader beforehand. If this service is done with small children, you may wish to shorten the Gospel reading or tell it in your own words.

Leader: When we were baptized, we promised to carry the flame of Christ's love into the world. We promised to reject sin and selfishness and to live as messengers of Christ's care in the human family. From time to time, we need to remind ourselves of our responsibilities. We need to renew our promises. We need to think about our actions to see how well we are living up to the challenge that our Baptism has given us. Let us listen to Christ's words as reminders of our call to be brothers and sisters in the human family.

Reader: "When the Son of Man comes in his glory, and all the angels with him, then he will sit on the throne of his glory. All the nations will be gathered before him, and he will separate people one from another as a shepherd separates the sheep from the goats, and he will put the sheep at his right hand and the goats at the left. Then the king will say to those at his right hand, 'Come, you that are blessed by my Father, inherit the kingdom prepared for you from the foundation of the world; for I was hungry and you gave me food, I was thirsty and you gave me something to drink, I was a stranger and you welcomed me, I was naked and you gave me clothing, I was sick and you took care of me, I was in prison and you visited me....Truly I tell you, just as you did it for one of these least who are members of my family, you did it to me.' "

Matthew 25:31-26, 40

Leader: Let us renew our baptismal commitment of believing in a loving, merciful God and of acting as loving, merciful brothers and sisters. Please repeat the prayer of faith after me:

I believe in one God, loving Creator and Protector of all.

I believe God has created me in the divine image, with dignity, beauty, and worth.

I believe in Jesus Christ, who showed His love in a life of sharing and a death of self-sacrifice.

I believe in the Holy Spirit of unity joining us together as one body.

Leader: Do you promise to feed the hungry and give drink to the thirsty?

All: I do.

Leader: Do you promise to welcome the stranger and clothe the naked?

All: I do.

Leader: Do you promise to care for the sick and visit the imprisoned?

All: I do.

Leader: Because we wish to renew our baptismal promises, we trace the Sign of the Cross on our foreheads. We belong to the Father, and to the Son, and to the Holy Spirit.

BIBLE PRAYER SERVICES
PRAYER IN PRAISE OF CREATION

This prayer can be used at any time to recall the wonders of God's creation and to be thankful to the Creator. A parent, grandparent, or teenager can lead the prayer. You may want to set the mood with a bouquet of flowers, a candle, or a special tablecloth. If possible, give the people who are leading or reading an opportunity to practice their parts before you hold the prayer service.

Leader: The Scriptures tell us that God is the Creator of everything and that God has made everything good. As we listen to the message of the creation story, let us be thankful for all of God's marvelous gifts to us.

Reader: In the beginning, when God began the creation, God said, "Let there be light" and there was light. God saw that the light was good. God separated the light from the darkness and called the light Day and the darkness Night. Then God gathered together the waters so that there would be dry land. God called the dry land Earth and the waters Seas. Again, God saw that the land and the waters were good. Then, at the command of God, the earth brought forth plants and trees of every kind. And God saw that all of them were good. Next, God set the lights in the dome of the sky— the sun, to give light to the day, and the moon, to give light to the night. God next created living creatures—animals of all kinds—to fill the waters and the sky and the land. God made all the living creatures good and told them to multiply and fill the earth. Finally, God created human beings, male and female, in God's own image and gave all the rest of the creation to the human beings with the charge to watch over it. God saw that everything created was very, very good.

Based on Genesis 1

Leader: Let us use the words of the psalm writer to express our gratitude to God for all of creation. Our response will be "Bless the LORD, O my soul!"

All: Bless the LORD, O my soul!

Leader: O LORD, my God, you are very great. You are clothed with honor and majesty, wrapped in light as with a garment.

All: Bless the LORD, O my soul!

Leader: You stretch out the heavens like a tent, you set the beams of your chambers on the waters, you make the clouds your chariot, you ride on the wings of the wind, you make the winds your messengers, fire and flame your ministers.

All: Bless the LORD, O my soul!

Leader: You set the earth on its foundations, so that it shall never be shaken. You cover it with the deep as with a garment; the waters stood above the mountains.

All: Bless the LORD, O my soul!

Leader: O LORD, how manifold are your works! In wisdom You have made them all; the earth is full of your creatures....

Psalm 104: 1-6, 24

All: Bless the LORD, O my soul!

Leader: Let us take a moment now to be thankful to God for all of creation. If you wish, you may mention something that you are especially thankful for today. You may simply say, "Today, I thank God for_____."

Leader: Let us pray: Creator God, You created the wonders of the world. The sun and the moon You set in place. You fashioned the rivers, the seas, the mountains, and the plains. You filled the world with fish and birds and animals of all kinds. Finally, You created humankind in Your own image. We are grateful for Your creative power. Thank You for making such a wonderful world, full of colors, sounds, and mystery. Thank You for creating a world of human community in which we are called to love one another. Help us be creators, too. May we take good care of Your creation and create a home of happiness and peace in this world. We ask this in the name of Jesus Christ, who is with us today and every day. Amen.

BIBLE PRAYER SERVICES
PRAYER FOR COOPERATION

This prayer can be used any time to help us focus on the importance of cooperation. A parent, grandparent, or teenager may lead the prayer. You will need a candle for each family member participating in the prayer and one additional candle to symbolize Jesus. You will also need a place to put each candle once it is lighted. You may wish to set the candles in a bowl of sand or in candle holders if you have enough of them. Gather around the kitchen or dining room table or a small table in the living or family room.

Leader: We light the candle in the middle of our table to symbolize Jesus Christ who is the light of our family. Without Christ we would be living in darkness. For He has shown us the way to God; He has shown us how to love. Let us listen to Jesus' challenge to be members of His body.

Reader: For just as the body is one and has many members, and all the members of the body, though many, are one body, so it is with Christ. For by one Spirit we were all baptized into one body—Jews or Greeks, slaves or free—and all were made to drink of one Spirit.

Indeed, the body does not consist of one member but of many. If the foot would say, "Because I am not a hand I do not belong to the body," that would not make it any less a part of the body. And if the ear would say, "Because I am not an eye, I do not belong to the body," that would not make it any less a part of the body. Now you are the body of Christ and individually members of it.

1 Corinthians 12:12-16, 27

Leader: As members of Christ's body, each one of us will light a candle from the Christ candle as a sign that we draw our life and light from Him. Then as each person places a lighted candle in the middle of the table, the other members of the family will mention gifts, talents, or qualities that they appreciate in this person.

During the candle lighting, you may wish to turn off the lights.

Leader: As members of the one body of Christ, let us pray for unity and understanding among our family and among the larger family of humankind. Our response to the prayers will be: God of love, hear our prayer.

Leader: Loving God, whenever we find anger or quarreling, may we be messengers of Your peace and cooperation, we pray:

All: God of love, hear our prayer.

Leader: Loving God, whenever we find sadness or sorrow, may we be messengers of Your healing and joy, we pray:

All: God of love, hear our prayer.

Leader: Loving God, whenever we find doubt or fear, may we be messengers of Your confidence and unlimited acceptance, we pray:

All: God of love, hear our prayer.

Leader: Loving God, whenever we find criticism or fighting, may we be messengers of Your unity and oneness, we pray:

All: God of love, hear our prayer.

Leader: Creator God, You have made us in Your image as members of the body of Christ. Give us the courage to be so united that we feel the pain and the joy of the other members of Christ's body. Help us understand the fears and doubts, the sorrow and sadness of those who have been hurt by others. Help us experience the joy and gladness of those who have experienced Your love through the care and cooperation of others. May we truly live as one body within our own family and within the larger family of Christ's body. May we be attentive to the needs of every member. May we be slow to anger and quick to forgive. May we be slow to criticize and quick to praise. We ask this in the name of Jesus, the Christ: Amen. Let us now join hands around this table and say the Lord's Prayer as members of His one body.

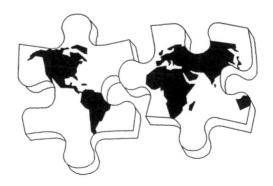

A PRAYER FOR HEARING

This prayer may be used at any time to focus on the importance of hearing God's voice in our daily lives. You may want to set the mood with a bouquet of flowers, a candle, or a special tablecloth. If possible, give the person who is reading the passage from the Bible an opportunity to practice the part.

Leader: Listen to the winds as they whisper through the treetops. Listen to the waters as they wash upon the shore. Listen to the voices of birds and animals that surround us. Listen to the voices of our human family, friends and enemies, children and seniors. Listen to the voice deep within. God speaks to us in many ways. We only need to listen.

Take a few minutes to listen to the world around you and the Spirit of God within you. If you wish, share what you hear. You may also wish to listen to a few minutes of quiet music or a recording of nature sounds.

Reader: At that time Eli, whose eyesight had begun to dim so that he could not see, was lying down in his room; the lamp of God had not yet gone out, and Samuel was lying down in the temple of the LORD, where the ark of God was. Then the LORD called, "Samuel! Samuel!" and he said, "Here I am!" and ran to Eli, and said, "Here I am, for you called me." But he said, "I did not call; lie down again." So he went and lay down. The LORD called again, "Samuel! Samuel!" Samuel got up and went to Eli, and said, "Here I am, for you called me." But he said, "I did not call, my son; lie down again." Now Samuel did not yet know the LORD, and the word of the LORD had not yet been revealed to him. The LORD called Samuel again, a third time. And he got up and went to Eli, and said, "Here I am, for you called me." Then Eli perceived that the LORD was calling the boy. Therefore Eli said to Samuel, "Go, lie down; and if he calls you, you shall say, 'Speak, LORD, for your servant is listening.'" So Samuel went and lay down in his place. Now the LORD came and stood there, calling as before, "Samuel! Samuel!" And Samuel said, "Speak, for your servant is listening."

1 Samuel 3:2-10

If you wish, discuss these or similar questions:

1. How does God call us or speak to us?

2. Describe a time when you felt called to respond to a challenge from God.

3. How can we be sure to be open to God's call?

Leader: Let us pray: God of amazing messages, open our ears to hear Your word. Help us listen to Your voice as You speak to us through the wonders of nature, the laws and guidance of the church, the love and challenge of those who care for us, and the longings for goodness and rightness in our own hearts. We ask this in the name of Jesus who lives forever and ever. Amen.

BIBLE PRAYER SERVICES
A CELEBRATION OF THE WORD

This prayer may be used as a meal prayer or as a special evening prayer. Any member of the family may lead the prayer and all should try to participate in the ritual as much as possible. A leader and reader will be needed for the prayer. If possible, give them a chance to practice their parts in advance. Gather the family around a table. You may wish to have an open Bible and candle in the middle of the table.

Leader: We come together to think about the message of Jesus and how we are called to be hearers of God's word. We must let the word of God take root in us so that we make it come alive in our daily actions. Just as Jesus lived a life of giving and love, we are called to give our lives for others. Let us listen to the challenge to be hearers with open ears.

Reader: When a great crowd gathered and people from town after town came to him, he said in a parable, "A sower went out to sow his seed; and as he sowed, some fell on the path and was trampled on, and the birds of the air ate it up. Some fell on the rock; and as it grew up, it withered for lack of moisture. Some fell among thorns, and the thorns grew with it and choked it. Some fell into good soil, and when it grew, it produced a hundredfold." As he said this, he called out, "Let anyone with ears to hear listen!

"Now the parable is this: The seed is the word of God. The ones on the path are those who have heard; then the devil comes and takes away the word from their hearts, so that they may not believe and be saved. The ones on the rock are those who, when they hear the word, receive it with joy. But these have no root; they believe only for a while and in a time of testing fall away. As for what fell among the thorns, these are the ones who hear; but as they go on their way, they are choked by the cares and riches and pleasures of life, and their fruit does not mature. But as for that in the good soil, these are ones who, when they hear the word, hold it fast in an honest and good heart, and bear fruit with patient endurance."

Luke 8: 4-8, 11-15

Leader: Let us pray to be good listeners and attentive hearers of the word. Please respond to the prayers with "Lord, may Your word take root in us."

Leader: Creator God, may our ears be open to hear Your word in the holy Scriptures. May we listen attentively to Your call for faith and action. We pray:

All: Lord, may Your word take root in us.

Leader: Creator God, may we also listen to Your word as it is spoken by others who guide us and care for us. May we hear Your call in the cries of the poor and the oppressed. We pray:

All: Lord, may Your word take root in us.

Leader: Creator God, when the thorns of life, the distractions and worries of this world, try to choke out Your word, may we have the courage to keep on listening to You. We pray:

All: Lord, may Your word take root in us.

Leader: Creator God, may Your word continue to grow in the soil of our lives. May it bear fruit in good works that serve the needy in our world. We pray:

All: Lord, may Your word take root in us.

Leader: Let us pray together as hearers of the word, that our ears and hearts may be open to the challenge of Christ.

All: Loving God, You have given us Your word as a seed to be planted in our hearts. Help us have ears that are open and hearts that are ready to hear Your voice. May we be good listeners to You and to each other, being especially attentive to the voice of the poor. When we hear Your challenge, may we be inspired to respond. Give us the courage to bear fruit in action. We ask this in the name of Jesus, Your risen Son. Amen.

To conclude the prayer, ask each person to put one hand on the Bible and say, "Lord, may Your word take root in me."

A PRAYER FOR LISTENING

This prayer may be used as a special meal prayer or evening prayer or after you have completed a family activity together. You may want to provide a lighted candle, tablecloth, flowers, or similar decorations that highlight the importance of the prayer time. You will need a leader and a reader for the prayer. Give them a chance to read over their part beforehand.

Leader: Creator God, we thank You for giving us the ability to listen and to speak. Open our ears to each other and to You. May we hear Your voice in the cry of the poor and lonely. May we listen to Your call in the sound of wind and rain. Help us take time to hear each other, to listen to the hopes, joys, and cares of all our brothers and sisters. We ask this in the name of Jesus who always listens to our prayers. Amen.

Reader: Let us listen to God's word in the Bible:
Wisdom cries out in the street, in the squares she raises her voice. At the busiest corner she cries out; at the entrance of the city gates she speaks...
...if you accept my words and treasure up my commandments within you, making your ear attentive to wisdom, and inclining your heart to understanding...
then you will...find the knowledge of God. For the Lord gives wisdom; from his mouth come knowledge and understanding; he stores up sound wisdom for the upright; he is a shield to those who walk blamelessly, guarding the paths of justice, and preserving the way of his faithful ones.

excerpts from Proverbs 1:20-21; 2:1-2,5-8

Leader: Let us give praise for the word that God gives us. Our response is based on Psalm 145: Lord, You are faithful in all Your words.

Leader: The LORD is faithful in all His words and gracious in all His works. The LORD upholds all who are falling and raises up all who are bowed down.

All: Lord, You are faithful in all Your words.

Leader: The eyes of all look to You, and You give them their food in due season; You open Your hand, satisfying the desire of every living thing.

All: Lord, You are faithful in all Your words.

Leader: The Lord is just in all His ways and kind in all His doings. The Lord is near to all who call on Him, to all who call on Him in truth.

All: Lord, You are faithful in all Your words.

Leader: Let us take a few moments now to listen in our own hearts to what God is saying to each one of us.

Allow a minute or two of silence or listen to a calming instrumental piece of music. If they wish, family members may share the messages that they heard in their own hearts as they listened to God.

Leader: We give You praise, Creator God, for being as close to us as the beating of own hearts. We thank You for giving us Your word to guide us. We thank You for listening to all of our prayers. We pray in the name of Jesus who hears us today and every day. Amen.

PRAYER FOR PEACE

This prayer may be used any time to help the family focus on the importance of being peacemakers. A parent, grandparent, or teenager may lead the prayer. You may wish to provide a candle and a small bouquet of flowers to set the atmosphere for prayer. In this prayer is a suggestion for sharing that you may wish to use if there is time. If you use the sharing time, mention the questions before you begin the prayer so that family members might have a chance to think about them ahead of time.

Leader: Creator God, You ask us to be peacemakers; to love one another. Help us treat each other as brothers and sisters. All together, we make up Your one family. Give us the courage to reach out our hands to each other when we are in need. May we never turn our backs on our neighbor. May we always live by the example of love that Jesus gave us. Listen to the prayers we speak to You now.

Reader: When we see others fighting or angry with each other, when we hear shouting or name-calling:

All: Help us be peacemakers.

Reader: When we feel like making fun of others because they do not think or act as we do:

All: Help us be peacemakers.

Reader: When we do something to make someone else unhappy, when we hurt someone by our words or actions:

All: Help us be peacemakers.

Reader: When we don't feel like helping, but we know we should:

All: Help us be peacemakers.

Reader: The Lord said: "Be holy, for I, your God, am holy. Do not steal. Do not lie or speak falsely to one another. You shall not act dishonestly. You shall not go about spreading rumors. You shall not hate your sisters or brothers, and this means all the people in our human family. Do not try to get even with others and don't hold a grudge against anyone. You shall love your neighbor as you love yourself. Listen to these words because I am your God."

Based on Leviticus 19:1-17

(If you wish, use the following questions for sharing.)

Leader: What kinds of things do peacemakers do? Would any of you like to share a time when you acted like a peacemaker? Are there any ways in which we might be a more peaceful family?

Leader: Let us join hands and say the Lord's Prayer together.

PRAYERS FOR HOLIDAYS
AND HOLY DAYS

PRAYERS FOR NEW YEAR

GOD OF CONSTANT CARE

God of constant care, we rejoice in Your promises to us. You have given us Your covenant, "I will walk among you, and will be your God, and you shall be my people." You have assured us with the words "I am with you always, to the end of the age." As we begin a new year, we know that You are with us every moment. You renew Your love for us with every sunrise. You are present to us with every breath we take. As we journey through this year, help us always recognize Your presence and constantly rejoice in Your love. This we ask in the name of Jesus, Your Son, who lives with You in the unity of the Holy Spirit, forever and ever. Amen.

PRAYER FOR PEACE

Creator God, as we begin this new year, help us treat each other as brothers and sisters. All together, we make up Your one family. Give us the courage to reach out our hands to each other when we are in need. May we never turn our backs on our neighbors. May we always live by the example of love that Jesus gave us. Make us Your peacemakers. May we bring Your peace to those who are lonely or without friends. May we bring Your peace to those who are hurting or feeling sad. May we bring Your peace to those who are angry or upset. Give us the courage to be messengers of Your peace. We ask this in the name of Jesus. Amen.

THE GIFT OF ANOTHER YEAR

God of life and light, You give us the gift of another year. Wrapped in hope and mystery, this gift calls us to put our trust in You. As we unwrap this precious gift day by day, may we live as grateful people. May we recognize Your presence in profound and simple moments, in ordinary and extraordinary events. Give us the insight to rejoice in the present moment, to accept its richness and its challenge. We make this prayer in the name of Jesus, who is with us today and every day. Amen.

THESE FORTY DAYS OF LENT

Creator God, You have fashioned us to be Your people, one family united in love. Throughout these forty days of Lent, may we listen to the cries of the poor. May we see the needs of those who are sick, lonely, and outcast. Give us the courage to call all people our brothers and sisters. May our lives reflect the love and sacrifice of Jesus. Send Your Holy Spirit upon us so that we might be a message of acceptance and joy to all we touch. We ask this in the name of Jesus, who has given us an example of perfect love. Amen.

LOVE AND SACRIFICE

As we begin this holy season of Lent, You challenge us, God of love, to look deeply at our lives. You ask us to recognize the needs of our fellow human beings and to respond to those needs with our love and sacrifice. Give us the courage to live as Jesus lived. May we see each other as Your creations, made in Your image and likeness. Help us believe with all our hearts and minds and strength that You love each one of us in the human family with an unconditional, constantly forgiving love. Creator God, You call us to follow You during this holy season of Lent, to be messengers of Your love. We promise to feed the hungry and give drink to the thirsty, to care for the sick and shelter the homeless. Give us the courage to be loving brothers and sisters to all of the members of our human family. Help us respond to their needs. We ask this in the name of Jesus, who teaches us how to love now and forever. Amen.

TO FOLLOW THE EXAMPLE OF JESUS

God of love, You sent Your son, Jesus, to show us the way, the truth, and the life. May we follow the example of Jesus, especially during this holy season of Lent. May we reach out our hands in service to others. May we use our voices to bring friendship and joy. May we use our minds to discover and learn. Help us realize how deeply You love each one of us. Help us understand that You are with us as we try to love as Jesus loved. We pray in the name of Jesus. Amen.

EASTER JOY

God, Our Creator, we thank You for Easter joy. Because of the resurrection of Jesus, we believe in new life. We have seen Your Son triumph over darkness and death, and so we have faith in Your promise that we will have a home with You forever. Inflame our hearts with Your Spirit of new life so that we might follow the example of Your Son, Jesus. By his life, death and resurrection, He has taught us how to love and forgive. Give us the courage to live for others as He did. Make us messengers of Your healing and peace. Open our minds and hearts by this Easter celebration and bring us one day to the celebration of eternal light. We ask this in the name of Jesus, our risen Lord, forever and ever. Amen.

NEW LIFE

Loving God, You raised Your Son, Jesus to new life. Help us see all of the ways in which You bring new life into our world. May we see Your love and power in the new life of springtime. May we recognize Your care for us in the smiles of friends and hugs of those who love us. May we have the courage to reach out for new life in friendship and sharing. We praise You, God of life, for bringing light out of darkness. May we live as children of Your light, showing forth Your love in our world. We ask this in the name of Jesus, the risen Lord: Amen.

YOU FIRST LOVED US

Loving God, on this day when we celebrate the resurrection of Jesus, we praise and thank You for life. We are able to live and love because You first loved us. You have loved us into life and You care for us throughout our days. You have prepared a place for each of us in that land of eternal love and justice, Your kingdom. May we live as members of that kingdom even now as we respond to Your challenge to love, not only our family and friends, but even our enemies. We ask this in the name of Jesus who has given us an example of perfect love. Amen.

A PRAYER FOR NEW BEGINNINGS

God, our Creator, every day is a new creation for us to live. We thank You for new beginnings. We thank You for the chance to learn new insights about Your world, to share our thoughts with new friends, to read new books, to sing new songs, and to praise You in a new season of our lives. Thank You for creating new beginnings once again for us. We praise You through Jesus Christ, who promises to journey with us on every new adventure. Amen.

A PRAYER FOR LEARNING

Creator God, there is so much to learn, so much to understand. Your world is full of wonder. We have only begun to understand the forces of nature and the laws of Your universe. We have only begun to understand the gifts that each person brings to the family of humankind. We have only begun to understand You in all Your greatness and love. Open our eyes and ears and hearts to appreciate more deeply the wonders of creation, the beauty of persons, and the mystery of Your love. As we begin a new year of learning, fill us with Your understanding. We ask this in the name of Jesus, Your Son. Amen.

SCHOOL PRAYER

God of all wisdom, send Your Spirit into my heart so that I might know You better. Give me clear sight to see Your powerful presence in my family, my school, and my world. Help me recognize Your image in my fellow learners so that together we might make one human family of brothers and sisters. Enlighten my mind with Your wisdom so that I might know the importance of learning and the challenge of living for others. We ask this in the name of Jesus, Your Son. Amen.

PRAYERS FOR THANKSGIVING

THANK YOU FOR THE GIFT OF LIFE

God of love, You are the Source of all life, all hope, all joy. We praise and thank You for the gift of life, for every heartbeat and every breath. We thank You for all Your promises and for a future that calls us forward. We thank You for the joy that we have in one another and in You. You have called us to be Your family of love and hope and joy. Help us be Your hands of care, touching one another's lives. May we be messengers of Your good news that

teaches us to hope for Your kingdom and to do Your will on earth. Open us to Your Spirit of joy that we might see all the blessings and gifts that surround us. Create in us a grateful spirit. May we be ever thankful so that we do not overlook Your gracious and abundant love in the everyday, extraordinary events of our lives. We thank You for loving us into being and for holding us close to Your heart. We thank You in the name of Jesus, who is our life, our hope and our joy, forever and ever. Amen.

WE GIVE YOU THANKS

God of goodness and mercy, we give You thanks and praise for the world You have created. We praise You for the trees that remind us to look to the heavens. We thank You for the waters that tell us of Your constant life-giving presence. We thank You for light and darkness, sun and moon, day and night. We praise You Creator God for the gift of the human family. We are grateful for people of all languages, creeds, and colors. Thank You for creating each one of us unique and precious in Your sight. We thank You for gathering us together at this place and time to praise You. May we never grow tired of praising Your goodness and remembering Your constant love. We thank You in the name of Jesus, who is with us now and promises to be with us forever. Amen.

A GRATEFUL PEOPLE

We praise and thank You, Creator God, for loving us into being, for giving us breath and spirit and life. We thank You for the uniqueness of every person, for individual gifts and talents. We thank You for those who have gone before us, who have tilled the soil and built the cities. We thank You for a future full of hope and a present full of challenge. May we always be a grateful people who recognize that with You we can do great things. Bless our family on this day. Keep us always in Your care. We ask this in the name of Jesus, who is with us today and everyday. Amen.

For many families, the lighting of the Advent wreath is a meaningful tradition that marks the progress of the season. If you do not have an advent wreath frame, you may simply set four candles in holders and surround them with a ring of greens. Some families gather around the Advent wreath once a week; others light the wreath every day for meal prayer or evening prayer. Whatever your family custom, you may wish to use these Advent wreath prayers.

FIRST SUNDAY OF ADVENT: Lord Jesus, as we begin this sacred season of joy and expectation, open our hearts to Your constant presence. May we be watchful and attentive to Your word made flesh in those around us. May we listen to the voice of the poor, to the cry of the lonely, to the unspoken hopes of those who feel crushed by life. Give us eyes to see You today and everyday. Amen.

SECOND SUNDAY OF ADVENT: Lord Jesus, shower us with Your Spirit. Give us the courage to live out the promises of our Baptism. May we be alive with Your word burning within us. May we speak of Your love with enthusiasm. Most important, help us be messengers of Your care to others. Give us strong and gentle hands to reach out to our sisters and brothers today and everyday. Amen.

THIRD SUNDAY OF ADVENT: Lord Jesus, help us prepare well for the celebration of Your birth and Your second coming. Keep us from being too wrapped up in the material things of this world. Set our eyes on the message of Christmas, a message of light and peace for the whole world. Help us find our way to forward Your kingdom and work toward Your peace on earth today and everyday. Amen.

FOURTH SUNDAY OF ADVENT: Lord Jesus, increase our faith so that we might believe that nothing is impossible with God. May we continue to be a people with dreams and visions of the possible—a human community of understanding and acceptance. May we be ready to risk as Mary did to make these dreams come true. Open us to know the power of Your presence today and everyday. Amen.

A PRAYER OF EXPECTATION

God of love and justice, we ask You to be among us as we pray together now so that we may see Your ever-present love and respond with hope and action. We rejoice because Your tender hands, like those of the potter, mold and shape our lives. We rejoice because You sent Your Son to show us the way to You. During this Christmas season, we ask Your help as we prepare a place in our world for Your justice. Help us be awake and attentive to every opportunity to share the love of Christ with others. Open our eyes to the needs of our brothers and sisters. Give us strength in body and spirit that we might carry the burdens of others. We ask this in the name of Jesus, who is our way, our truth, and our life, forever and ever. Amen.

THE FEAST OF THE EPIPHANY–VISIT OF THE WISE MEN

Creator God, as we celebrate the visit of the three wise men to the child Jesus, help us see more clearly the gifts that we can bring to the manger. Help us recognize that all of our talents and abilities are gifts from You. May we return our gifts to You by using them properly, by reaching out in service to others, and by continuing to develop our talents. We ask this in the name of Jesus, who is Your most wonderful gift to us. Amen.

IN HUMAN FLESH

God of love, we celebrate Your presence among us in Christmas joy. In Jesus, You have come into our history, into our human life. You are not a god who lives in the distance or stands apart from our lives. Rather, You took on human flesh to make Your home here among us. We thank You, God, for the gift of Jesus. May we praise You throughout this holy season and throughout our lives as we see the signs of Your unending love for us. Help us live in the light of Christ. When it is dark, we stumble and we are afraid. When it is light, we can see clearly. We have no need for fear, and we can see where to go. In Jesus You have given us Your gift of light. Now, we face the challenge to be a light for others. Shower us with Your Spirit that we might understand how we can best use our talents and gifts to bring Your light into the world. Strengthen us with Your courage that we might take the risk to respond to those who are in need of food, shelter, comfort and care. Lord of Light, inflame our hearts with the fire of Your love that we might always be sensitive to the voices of the poor and the oppressed. We ask this in the name of Jesus, the true light who has come into our world. Amen.

LABOR DAY

Loving God, we thank You for all those people who do their jobs every day with dedication and care. For farmers who grow their crops so that we might eat. For bakers who rise early to make our daily bread to feed us. For architects, engineers, plumbers, electricians, and all those who plan and build our homes, hospitals, schools, and businesses. For the leaders of our Church and country who try to guide us with fairness and insight. We pray for all those who work to serve the needs of our human family. Keep each of us in Your care and lead us one day to Your kingdom of eternal peace. We ask this in the name of Jesus, who lives forever and ever. Amen.

MEMORIAL DAY

Loving Father, we remember all those who have gone before us believing in freedom for all. May they find peace in Your loving embrace, a kingdom of perfect justice. May we live out the ideals and hopes in which they believed and for which they sacrificed. We offer You all that we are. May our thoughts, our work, and our words give You praise and thanks. May our lives show forth Your love and care. Let us see our world with Your eyes of understanding. Let us hear the voices of those who are asking for help. Give us the courage to share our lives, our time, and our gifts so that others may find greater joy. We offer You all that we have in Jesus' name. Amen.

FOURTH OF JULY

God of love, we pray for our country on this day of independence. We pray that our country will always be a land of the free, where people of every race, creed, and color will be able to live in peace. Creator God, Your care has no boundaries, Your love has no end. May Your justice be a way of life for all people. May all Your family learn to live in peace. We pray this in the name of Jesus, who has taught us how to love. Amen.

MARTIN LUTHER KING, JR., ANNIVERSARY

Holy God, You create every person in Your own image and likeness. Because Your Holy Spirit lives within us, we are all brothers and sisters. Today, we remember our brother, Martin Luther King, Jr., who worked so tirelessly to proclaim that all Your people are equal. We remember his  powerful message about the dignity and worth of every human being. Holy God, help us live as one family, rejoicing in our common bonds and respecting our differences. We ask this in the name of Jesus, Your Son. Amen.

PARENTING INSIGHTS

NEW YEAR RESOLUTIONS FOR THE CHURCH

As we reflect on our needs and hopes for the new year, it might be good to think about the larger family to which we belong—the church family. Although there are many things any one of us can identify as challenges for personal improvement, we also need to recognize the part we play in supporting and nourishing the larger community of faith. Losing weight, arguing less, helping with homework more, spending more time in prayer or Scripture reading, striving for greater patience, reading regularly are examples of the kinds of personal goals we might set for ourselves as we look at the year ahead. However, we are also challenged to look at our life in the larger community and to ask ourselves how we can be more supportive members of the church.

Involvement in the church with our families gives our children a sense of belonging to a larger family. This involvement communicates to our children a clear message that we believe we have responsibilities to all members of the human family. The challenge of faith-filled living involves responding to needs and issues that go far beyond our personal lives or the lives of our family members.

It would be impossible to list all of the ways persons might become more involved in their church family. However, if we reflect on a few of the primary missions or goals of the church, we will find ourselves being challenged to more active participation. One of the primary ways of understanding *church* is as a community, as a people of God. When we think of this definition of *church*, we are challenged to develop a greater sense of belonging and care for each other. We might ask ourselves if there are ways we can get to know better some of the other members of our church. Should we be participating in the social life of our church more regularly? Do the members of our church community have needs with which we might be able to help?

Another understanding of *church* is as a messenger of good news in the world. The church is called to speak the Gospel message powerfully and clearly in every age. As members of the messenger church, we are challenged to proclaim the Gospel of Jesus Christ to others. This might involve us in witnessing to our fellow workers, in teaching others in Christian education classes, or in leading discussion groups on the Scriptures. There are many ways in which we are invited to take an active role in being a messenger of the Gospel, both formally and informally.

A final way of understanding *church* that challenges us to involvement is to see the church as a servant in the world. From this perspective the church is summoned to address the needs of the poor, lonely, homeless, hungry, and oppressed throughout our globe. When we think of the church as servant, we are challenged to take a more active role in social concerns. How can we become involved in programs of direct help for those who are less fortunate in our world? Are there meal programs, homeless shelters, free clinics, and other similar places where we could volunteer to fulfill the church's call to be a servant in the world? Are there elderly neighbors, shut-ins, handicapped, grieving persons who need help with physical chores or just an ear to listen? We must also look at the structures and institutions within our society that oppress others. What can we do to change these unjust structures and systems? Are there ways in which we are being challenged to become involved in the political process to bring about more just laws and policies?

Clearly, there are more than enough jobs to go around. When we look at the challenges that our church faces, we are sometimes overwhelmed by the immensity of the task. It is important for us to recall Paul's message that each one of us is an integral part of the Body of Christ. Each one of us is an important member and has a significant role to fulfill. Just as there are feet and eyes and fingers in the human body, each with its own function, so in the Body of Christ there are people with different talents and gifts. Only when all the parts of the body work together is there a fully-functioning and healthy body. So it is with the church. Only when all the members of the church work together—to be a community, a messenger of good news, and a servant in the world—can the church begin to fulfill its mission. We, as adults, must become convinced of the importance of every member of the body. If we can pass this message to our children, they will come to see their important role as part of the Body of Christ.

PRAYER AND ACTION FOR LENT

Toward the end of Matthew's Gospel, there is a familiar parable that, in many ways, sums up the life of Jesus and the challenge of the Christian. It is the parable of the last judgment at which the king separates the sheep from the goats. He says to the sheep, "Come, you that are blessed by my Father, inherit the kingdom prepared for you from the foundation of the world; for I was hungry and you gave me food, I was thirsty and you gave me something to drink, I was a stranger and you welcomed me, I was naked and you gave me clothing, I was sick and you took care of me, I was in prison and you visited me" (Matthew 25: 34-36).

Jesus lived His life for others. He gave everything, even His life. The penitential season of Lent asks us to reflect on our lives to see how they match His. Whose hunger have we fed; whose thirst have we satisfied? When was the last time we welcomed a stranger? Whom have we clothed recently? Have we cared for the sick and the imprisoned? In short, have we given up our lives so that others might experience life more fully?

One of the marvelous mysteries that comes to light in the resurrection experience is that when we give up our lives, we receive new life–abundant and overflowing. The message of the Easter season is that whenever we share our life as Jesus did, we will experience even greater life and joy.

This lesson of death and resurrection is a key principle for us, as parents, to teach our children. They will learn this lesson most easily and most surely by seeing us and participating with us in giving time, talent, and treasures to those in need. They will witness the joy, the satisfaction, and the new relationships that flow into our lives when we give up our lives for others. They will experience this new life along with us if they participate in service to others.

A vibrant faith life includes both prayer and action, reflection and service. The season of Lent and Easter is an important time to consider the balance of these two elements of faith in your family. How is your personal prayer life? How is your family prayer life? Do you set aside some time on a consistent basis for prayer? Have you made prayer part of the fabric of your family life? How are you serving others, sharing your time, talent, and treasures with the needy?

The life of faith involves these two elements–faith and action–because they support and sustain one another. Prayer gives us opportunities to hear God's call, God's challenge to be for others. Prayer also gives us the chance to simply bask in the warmth of the Creator's presence and voice our praise. In prayer, we put our efforts in perspective in relation to God's wisdom and future kingdom. Without prayer, we would soon tire of our activities and service, which often do not bear fruit as we envisioned.

Christian service and action puts flesh on the bones of faith. It is the concrete enactment of our belief that all are created in the image and likeness of God. Christian service is our response to the parable of Matthew, which would have us see the needs of the hungry, thirsty, homeless, sick, and imprisoned in our community.

If we are going to nurture family faith, we must participate in prayer and action. We must be able to celebrate and reflect on the Gospel. We must spend time listening to God's voice. We must also serve the needs of our fellow family members. We must translate the word of the Gospel into flesh, into action that brings new life and abundant joy.

LENT: SEASON OF PENANCE AND SACRIFICE

The season of Lent is a penitential season, a season of sacrifice. Often we have interpreted penance and sacrifice as "giving something up." The important thing, however, is that our penance or sacrifice helps us grow spiritually. It does little good for us to give up a television show or candy treats or dessert if our sacrifice does not help us understand more clearly what we are called to be and to do as followers of Jesus. Penance should help us reorient our lives to God. The focus of God's kingdom is quite different from the focus of the kingdom of this world. There are many indications that our contemporary Western society is focused on the making and spending of money. The kingdom of God, however, is focused on sharing the resources of the earth so that all have their needs met. It is easy for us and our children to get caught up in the accumulation of wealth or the purchase of the latest gadgets and luxuries. Commercials constantly attempt to seduce us into thinking that we need a particular type of clothing, car, or perfume in order to be popular, successful, or happy. However, if we focus our lives on the challenge of Jesus, we are called to support the dignity of every person. Our actions and sacrifices must address the basic needs of others for food, clothing, shelter, water, self-respect, and love.

Doing penance should help us put our priorities in order. The best kind of penance or sacrifice will (a) raise our consciousness, (b) help us be thankful, and (c) do good in the world. Let's consider each of these elements.

A. **RAISE OUR CONSCIOUSNESS.** Penance should help us understand more deeply the needs of our brothers and sisters and how we might best respond to these needs. In a sense, there is an educational element to penance. Through fasting, we might recognize personally the pain of going hungry. Through sacrificing a want we have, we might see more clearly the needs of our brothers and sisters. As we do acts of penance during the Lenten season, we need to couple these sacrifices with a deeper understanding of the needs of others. It would be good to find out about the homeless or hungry in your own community or in the world.

B. **HELP US BE THANKFUL.** Penance should help us be grateful for the gifts that we have been given. This attitude of gratefulness will help us live with a positive and helpful spirit. When we are grateful people, we stop taking things for granted. Penance should not make us gloomy or grumpy. Rather, it should enable us to realize the blessings in our own lives.

C. **DO GOOD IN THE WORLD.** Finally, our penance should be helpful to us or to others. Giving up something just for the sake of giving it up has little meaning. If we decide to give up family desserts twice a week, our sacrifice would be meaningful if, for example, we saved the money these desserts would cost, and contributed it to a good cause. If we give up watching a particular television program, our sacrifice would be meaningful if we spent the time writing letters, reading a spiritual book, or spending some time with the family. The focus of our penance should be to help us hear and respond to the challenge of Jesus. Penance should help us consider our priorities and change our hearts where needed.

Forgiveness is one of the most profound forms of love. Our forgiveness of our children frees them from the past. Forgiveness allows them to face new circumstances and decisions without a burden of guilt.

Forgiveness does not mean that there are no consequences for actions or no punishments for bad choices. It is very important for parents to provide discipline that inculcates a firm set of values and principles. Without such discipline, children have no sense of direction for shaping their own responses to life's questions. Consistency in discipline lays the foundation for morality and ethics in later life. Discipline and forgiveness go hand in hand. A punishment is given as a response to a wrong action or decision. Forgiveness is given as a response to the child. Through forgiveness, we say to our children, "We love you. A wrong decision or a bad action doesn't make you bad."

Here are some suggestions for sharing forgiveness, this very important gift of love. First, forgiveness needs to be said loudly and clearly. Don't just presume that the person knows. The words "I forgive you" are powerful expressions of love.

Second, try to talk about the feelings that are frequently a part of misunderstandings or arguments. If we do not have an opportunity to express our feelings, they often fester and breed hostility. Take the time to sit down with everyone involved and sort out the feelings surrounding the experience.

Third, celebrate forgiveness. A hug, a flower, a family treat might be used to express forgiveness. Choose a ritual or gesture that fits your family and says, "Let's put this behind us and start over."

EASTER FAITH

 *Faith* has many meanings. Often people use this word to refer to the creed, those core beliefs that have been held by followers of Jesus throughout the ages. Others interpret faith as a set of moral guidelines by which they chart the course of their actions. Still others refer to faith as trust, having confidence in God's goodness and love. Although these ideas are aspects of the experience of faith, they fail to get to the root reality. Faith may be expressed intellectually in creeds and moral codes, but these beliefs and guidelines are really the outgrowth of faith. Although faith may be expressed emotionally in trust or confidence, these convictions spring from faith. Fundamentally, faith is a way of seeing. Faith is the way we look at the world.

In this sense, everyone has faith. Every person sees the world in a particular way. We might say that everyone sees reality through a particular pair of lenses that color what they see. Some people look out at the world and see the presence and power of God. Others see a bleak and deteriorating world. Followers of Jesus are people of hope, people who see new life happening. This doesn't mean that Christians are naive optimists who ignore the evil in the world. Rather, Christians are people who recognize death and darkness but know that this isn't the end. Christians see the gift of God's life and love breaking through even the deepest darkness.

As a way of seeing, faith is really caught–not taught. The creedal statements and the moral guidelines can be taught. However, faith as a way of seeing comes from being shown the world from a particular viewpoint. As parents, we are responsible for showing our children the world of light and hope. We do this in a thousand little ways–by being thankful for a new day, by laughing in the midst of difficulties, by looking on the bright side, by forgiving others because they are made in God's image. We pass on our faith whenever we proclaim God's powerful action in our lives–when we see a coincidence as God's blessing and a positive turn of events as a sign of God's presence.

The core of Christian faith is the resurrection. Through the resurrection of Jesus, we see that death is not the end. We see that God brings light out of darkness, life out of death, and hope out of despair. We pass on our faith when we help our children see the new life that is happening all around us, whether that be in the flowers of springtime or the forgiveness that conquers hurt.

As you celebrate Lent and Easter with your family, may you be attentive to the new life that is happening in the world and in the hearts of faithful people everywhere. Show your children a world filled with God's presence, power, and love. Help your children feel the brightness and the warmth of living in God's wonderful creation, in the circle of light.

SUMMER: A SEASON FOR WONDER

 Religious experience begins in wonder. The experience of the wonder-full opens us to the ultimate mystery of God. When we wonder at the world and at one another, we begin to see the power of God's presence around and within us. We recognize that something more than physical processes and natural events are at work in our world and in ourselves.

Any time is a good time for wonder. The posture of wondering needs to become a habit or attitude with which we view life. However, the summer season seems to be a particularly appropriate time for wonder. As we take time away from our usual hectic schedules, we may slow down enough to notice a little more of the profound beauty that surrounds us. Many take time for a walk in the woods, a bike ride through the park or some star gazing. For most of us, summer is a time when our attention to the beauty of nature and to the preciousness of our families is heightened.

Since wonder is the source of religious experience, we parents need to teach our children to wonder. Actually, it seems that wonder comes naturally. Our children already know how to wonder. If you have ever listened to the constant questions of a three-year-old, you know that wondering seems to be a universal God-given talent. We simply need to be sure that no roadblocks stand in the way of the experience of wonder.

So how can we, as families, open ourselves to the mystery of God and religious experience? We can take the simple steps, Stop, Look, Listen. First we need to stop our hectic pace. We need to take time out of our regular routine. Perhaps we need to set aside some days for vacation. We may need to schedule into our week some family time for walking, biking, hiking, picnicking, gardening, visiting, talking, and listening. In a society that offers us so many opportunities for activity and involvement, one of the major challenges is to avoid over-scheduling ourselves or our children. We need to find a balance between activity and wonder. Some of our time should be unstructured. We need to learn to be open to the moment before us.

Second, we need to look. We need to notice the sun shining through the branches of an oak tree, the smile of a young child, the beauty of flowers. If we are attentive to the world in which we live, we see clearly the power and the beauty of God. In every grain of sand, shape of leaf, color of rainbow, we find revealed the loving hand of a Creator God.

Finally, we need to listen, to open our ears to the voices within our families and our communities. Hearing is an occasion of wonder. In listening to another, we recognize the precious image of God reflected in the person's gifts and concerns. When we open our ears to others, we begin to see the mystery that is at work in the life of every person. We wonder at the wisdom and insight of others.

When we stop, look, and listen, we will wonder at the profound beauty and mystery that surrounds us and is within us. When we stop, look, and listen, we will experience the presence and power of a loving God who is constantly with us.

ADVENT/CHRISTMAS: A TIME TO CREATE TRADITIONS

The way we celebrate Advent and Christmas will create memories and attitudes that will outlast any other gift we might give our children during this holiday season. The traditions experienced and remembered from childhood are usually treasured and imitated. Traditions give our children a connection with the past that provides roots for them and also a sense of confidence about the future.

Tradition connects us to a story that is larger than our own. When we use rituals and tell stories that come from ethnic or family customs, we gain a sense of being part of history. We see the importance of our lives as a continuation of the chain of generations that have lived before us. As we recognize our connectedness to the past, we deepen our feeling of responsibility. Just as others have worked and created before us, so we are challenged to work and create today. The chain of life and meaning depends upon the present generation carrying on from the past. We are called to take the best from our ancestors–their wisdom, principles, stories, meanings–and communicate these to future generations.

Tradition can instill a feeling of confidence about the future as well. When we see that other persons have already struggled through the difficulties of life, we can gain a stronger assurance about our own abilities. Just as others have endured the hardships of sickness, death, and broken relationships, so we will be able to turn the crises of our lives into opportunities for growth.

In our style of celebrating Advent and Christmas, we communicate our basic values and priorities to our children. In a sense, we help them create an understanding of Christmas and of life that will be part of them for the rest of their lives.

Let the activities, sights, sounds, and prayers of this holiday season create a tradition that will nourish your children's sense of rootedness in the past and confidence in the future.

CHRISTMAS: DOLLARS AND SIGNS

 For most parents, financial matters are a significant concern for at least three reasons: (1) There never seems to be quite enough money to buy all the things that we need. (2) We wish our kids had a greater sense of responsibility about money. (3) As we consider our brothers and sisters who are less fortunate, we know that we are called to share our resources with them. Especially at Advent and Christmas time, which has become a very materialistic season for many, this topic of financial resources is very important.

How we answer the three concerns mentioned above and act on them will have an important effect on how our children view dollars and signs. How we use our money is one of the most significant signs of our true priorities in life. Discuss this topic with your children, if you feel comfortable doing so. Such a discussion can be an extremely important lesson for them. But even if you do not discuss it with them, your actions will speak loudly and clearly of your priorities. Let's look closely at the three concerns that have been raised.

1. There never seems to be enough money to buy all the things that we need. What is the difference between a need and a want? Go around your house and take an inventory of your possessions. What things fall into the category of needs, and what things fall into the category of wants? Help your children understand the crucial difference between these two categories and the fact that many of our brothers and sisters are needy in the most desperate sense of that term.

2. We wish our kids had a greater responsibility about money. In order to understand how to be financially responsible, children need to see role models making decisions about money. If the topic of finances is a secret one, it is very difficult for the children to comprehend the importance of these decisions or the struggles involved in making them. Your children need not be informed of every detail of the family economy. However, it may be instructive for them to understand how the budget is divided. If you use the analogy of a pie, first graders and on can understand that three pieces of the pie pay for the house, one piece goes to taxes to pay for schools and social programs, and so on.

3. As we consider our brothers and sisters who are economically poor, we know that we are called to share our resources with them. Recognizing that our own needs are generally fulfilled, we need to look at our budget and see how we can realistically respond to the survival needs of some of our brothers and sisters. Although often our response may take the form of financial support, we are challenged to respond with our talents and time as well. This season of Advent and Christmas may give us the opportunity to consider how we are using our time, talent, and treasure to bring joy and hope to others. When we become involved as a family in giving of ourselves, we learn the most important lesson of this holy season of expectation—that we meet the Lord in our fellow human beings.

CHRISTMAS: THE GIFT OF SELF

As our families prepare for Christmas, many of our thoughts and much of our time is taken up with gifts. We hope to find just the right gift for grandparents or uncles and aunts. In some families, the children make a list of their wishes. In other families, members pick names and exchange gifts with one another. We use gifts to tell others how much we appreciate them and wish them every good thing.

A familiar saying is "The best gift is the gift of oneself." In many ways we, in our culture, seem to have forgotten the truth behind these words. There is so much emphasis on getting the latest toys and gadgets that few people even try to give a gift of themselves. Many people spend innumerable hours of time and a tremendous amount of money buying the most recent fashions and appliances, only to find themselves exhausted and worried about the bills when Christmas arrives. In the rush and spending, little thought is given to the "gift of self." Yet, if we examine our memories, it is often the simple gift made by hand that stands out as most important, most deeply an expression of love. Often it is the gift of time spent with someone in a special activity or event that seems to speak more loudly and surely of that person's care than all the material gifts in the world.

During this season of holy preparation for the celebration of the birth of Christ, ask yourself if there are ways you can give the gift of yourself. Take some time during these weeks leading up to December 25 to create personal expressions of your care and thankfulness. Help members of your family use their talents and time to express their love for others in ways that will touch the hearts of those who receive their gifts. You may find that giving the gift of self is also more satisfying for the whole family. Creating the gifts can become a fun and exciting time in itself. Here are some simple suggestions for "gifts of oneself."

There is no more precious commodity in the whole world than time. When we spend time with others, we are telling those persons how valuable and worthwhile they are, how much they really mean to us. An excellent "gift of self" is the gift of time. You may wish to make a homemade card or gift certificate with markers, crayons, finger paints, or other materials, with a promise to spend time with the person in a particular activity that both of you enjoy. Gifts of self might include time for planting flowers together in spring, time to picnic in a favorite park, time to watch the birds at a wildlife refuge, time to go to the zoo together, time to spend at the beach in the coming summer, time to bake cookies, time to go to the movies or fishing, time to can pickles or make jam, time to visit a museum together. Time spent together is truly a gift of oneself. Give some thought to how you might spend time with those you love. What activities, events, adventures, or hobbies would the other person or family enjoy?

Another way to share the gift of yourself is to use your talents and special abilities to make something for others. Write a story or poem. Do cross-stitch or embroidery. Paint a picture or build a shelf. Bake some special cookies or make an ornament for the tree. Create a custom-designed T-shirt or sweatshirt with acrylic paints. Build a flower box, a birdhouse or a lawn ornament. Knit a scarf. Letter a meaningful saying and frame it. There are many ways to share the gift of yourself. Be sure to begin early on your projects and keep them simple.

Gift Certificate

ONE DAY AT THE ZOO

If gifts of time and talent are new ideas for your family or for other relatives, you will need to find a balance with the more traditional forms of gift-giving. However, take the risk to give the gift of yourself. The central message of Christmas is that God cared enough to give us God's very being in the flesh and blood of a newborn baby in Bethlehem. If we follow God's example, the best Christmas gift is the gift of self.

COOPERATION: THE COMMON GOOD

There is a renewed emphasis in our society today on the art of cooperation. More and more businesses have recognized the need for teamwork and employee participation as they have responded to the need for higher quality products. Programs for quality improvement often rely on the wisdom and insight that comes from cooperative problem-solving.

In education as well, many teachers have begun to use cooperative learning strategies, which emphasize the sharing of ideas and talents in small groups. This student-centered style of learning recognizes that children can learn a great deal from each other. The future of our society depends on persons working together toward common goals. More than ever before, persons are aware that we are all members of a global village. If we are to survive, we will need to understand each other and work together in cooperation.

The cooperative strategies being used in business and education today underline the importance of the central Christian realization that all of us are brothers and sisters. We belong to the same family. Each of us has been created in the image and likeness of God. Each of us is challenged to use our particular gifts and talents to build up the community.

The family is the first and most important teacher of this central Christian value of cooperation. We learn to recognize and cherish the preciousness of others by listening to the insights and understanding the perspectives of those with whom we live. We learn the skills of cooperation by working together as members of one family.

How can we as parents help our children learn this core Christian teaching? First, we can model a cooperative spirit and way of living. Do our children see us acting cooperatively with spouse, friends, relatives, fellow workers, and fellow church members? Do our children witness our involvement in activities that build up the community—whether those be church-related or political or civic? If we can answer "yes" to these two questions, we have a good start on modeling a cooperative life-style for our children.

Second, we can practice cooperation within the family. This means listening to the various perspectives of family members as we make decisions. It means using the talents and gifts of family members in getting work done and problems solved. It means calling a family meeting to decide important issues. It means relying on the contributions of all family members in creating a home.

When we practice cooperation, we soon come to recognize that we are enriched by the diversity of perspectives, by the different insights of others. We come to realize that together we can do things that we were not able to do alone. In fact, it becomes apparent that in cooperating, we gain new insights and new solutions that are beyond our individual contributions.

If we are going to lead our family to greater cooperation, we need to be open. Cooperation requires that we come to discussion without having our minds made up. It means that we will consider seriously a perspective different from our own. It means we will take the risk to try a way with which we might not totally agree.

Cooperation also takes time. It is often easier and quicker to do something ourselves than to have young children involved. It takes patience to watch a young child repeatedly try something that is second nature to us. It takes time to listen to the needs and wishes of all family members. It takes time to discuss issues and come to mutually agreeable solutions. It takes time to work together and share our talents with each other. But when we believe that all of us are members of the one body and that every member of that body is of equal value, then cooperation will become a way of life for us.

RESPECT FOR NATURE

A very important value to instill in our children is a love and respect for nature. Children naturally wonder about the beauty and complexity of creation. As parents, we should nourish that sense of wonder that leads to appreciation and gratitude for all that God has created.

Over the past twenty years, there has been a significant change in the Christian attitude toward nature. For centuries our tradition took the perspective that human beings were to "multiply, and fill the earth and subdue it" (Genesis 1:28), as some translations of the creation story put it. In other words, we looked at nature as something that was supposed to serve us, something that could be used to fulfill our needs and wants. That attitude of being dominant over the earth has played a significant role in bringing us to a real ecological crisis today. The new attitude of the Church is one of living in harmony with nature rather than in domination over it.

Our children need to learn at an early age that they have a responsibility to protect the natural world, to respect the life of plants and animals that together with us make up the interconnected community of earth.

This attitude of living in harmony with nature can best be passed on by simply taking time to appreciate water, air, flowers, trees, and animals. Take time to notice wild flowers growing in a field, and then try to identify them. Listen to the songs of the birds. You may want to build a birdhouse or put a feeder out for some of our feathered friends. Go for a leisurely walk in the park. Take the family camping in a state park or forest. Many state and federal parks have naturalists who offer entertaining and educational hikes and programs. Paddle a canoe down one of our land's wondrous rivers. You might even begin in your own backyard by planting a garden or some flowers. Remember to celebrate the first bright blossom or the first ripe tomato because all of nature is God's gift to us.

Our survival and that of our children ultimately depends on how well we establish a mutually beneficial relationship with nature. We need to be friends with the natural environment around us. This attitude is best developed in a simple and natural way when a person is young.

THE ART OF LISTENING

The most important art in developing any relationship is the art of listening. It is through listening that we come to know another person. We come to understand the preciousness of another by hearing about that person's dreams and hopes, concerns and fears, triumphs and failures. However, this is only one way of looking at listening. In this way, listening is seen as a source for information, a way of gaining knowledge. Although this aspect of listening is certainly important, it is not the most significant aspect of listening.

The most important reason why listening is at the heart of any developing relationship is that the act of listening tells the other person that we care. When we listen to another person, we are saying to that individual, "You are important. You are so important that I will give you my undivided attention." Listening is a way of showing respect and love.

One of the greatest challenges of parenthood is making the time to listen to our children. We have devised all kinds of ways of listening without really listening. Some parents actually think they can read the paper or watch TV or sort through coupons while they are listening. It doesn't work. We know it and our children know it. Everyone's schedule these days is overflowing with too much to do and too many places to go. We need to stop and put listening on the priority list of things to do, and home on the priority list of places to go. Remember, listening is not so important for what we might learn. Its real importance is the message that listening gives to our children. When we give our children our undivided attention, they are getting the message that they are precious and loved. We aren't just *saying* they are important; we are *proving* it by taking the time to hear them. By listening, we say, "I care about what happened to you today. I care about the concerns that you have. You and your experiences are important to me."

Listening involves more than hearing the words of our children. It also entails reading the nonverbal messages that they send. Often the bigger part of the message comes through their facial expressions, the way they hold their heads, their tone of voice. Read between the lines. Get the whole message. However, the message we send by listening to our kids is the most important message of all.

ATTITUDE TOWARD THE NEW

As parents, we are often in a position to calm the fears of our children who are facing new friendships, new schools, new teachers, and new experiences in life. We can encourage creativity, inventiveness, and a positive attitude toward the new. These skills and attitudes are extremely important both from a human and a religious perspective.

From a human perspective, adaptation and change is a constant of life. Our survival as a species in the long run depends on our ability to respond to new situations and to create new structures of cooperation with our fellow human beings. As we become more deeply aware of the limited resources of our planet and the extent to which we have damaged our earth, an attitude of creative cooperation is critical. We must teach our children to come up with new answers, to have a broader vision, to be pioneers of new systems and new technologies.

From a spiritual perspective, the constant challenge of the Christian is to apply core values and a tested tradition to an ever-changing age. The Word of God is creative and transforming, pulling us forward toward the future reign of God. It is a Word that actively promotes justice and peace among all persons, a Word of hope and vision. We must teach our children to listen to this Word and to act on it. We need a new generation of Christians who are excited about the possibilities of transforming the world in creative response to the Word of God.

It is critical that the skills of creativity, inventiveness, and visioning be practiced with children. As with any skill, these skills are learned through doing. Simply put, we must give our children opportunities to think new thoughts, try out new ideas, make inventions, and look into the future. Children at any age can draw, paint, sculpt, and make up stories with their creative talents. They can design and make birdhouses, lawn ornaments, doll clothes, and space stations. They can create new recipes. As parents, we don't always have to give our children the answers. When we come upon a problem, we can ask our children to work it out. We can give them practice at being creators of the new.

How Do You Play Peace???

This is a question worth considering. We learn a great deal through play. As children we spend considerable energy learning information and practicing skills that will be important to us as adults. If we reflect on many of our models for organized recreation, education, and play, we might be struck by the competitiveness of our society. We don't seem to know how to play peace.

Beginning at an early age, we play *against* another person or team. The winners get rewarded with congratulations and sometimes trophies. Parents on the sidelines often talk as if winning the game is a matter of life or death. We push our children to compete harder and win more often. If you listen to the comments of the players before and during the game, you will hear action words such as *kill*, *smash*, *hit*, *crush*, and *beat*. On the one hand, children certainly are not speaking literally when they use this language. On the other hand, this kind of language contains an implicit message that is communicated to our children through much organized recreation.

Many models of education, from kindergarten onward, reward competitiveness. In the majority of classrooms, education is something students do *against* their classmates rather than *with* them. Students are required to do assignments, projects, and tests on their own. Independence is praised. Teamwork is often not encouraged. The skills of cooperation and collaboration are rarely practiced.

Most of the television shows that our children watch are permeated with violence. The prime-time shows are filled with shootings, knifings, and bombings. Even the cartoons rely on violence to make us laugh. News broadcasts and newspapers carry story after story about war, physical and sexual abuse, and other violent crimes.

With all of these influences, it is not surprising that more and more students are becoming violent. How do we counteract these influences? We need to play peace at an early age. We need to reward compassion, humility, and cooperation. We need to practice saying we're sorry. We need to model for our children a style of life that says it is more important to have fun than to win. We need noncompetitive games and activities as well as competitive ones. We need to reward people for who they are— special and unique—and not always for winning.

If we do not play peace more often with our children, the world is destined for more warfare and strife. Diplomacy, collaboration, and conflict resolution are adult activities that rest on the basic attitudes and values of a person. The foundational values for these adult activities are learned at an early age by playing peace.

INDEX